Inclusion:
Strategies for Working with
Young Children

A Resource Guide for Teachers,
Childcare Providers,
and
Parents

Lorraine O. Moore, Ph.D.

Peytral Publications, Inc.
Minnetonka, Minnesota

Inclusion: Strategies for Working with Young Children
                                                    by Lorraine O. Moore

Published by:
        Peytral Publications, Inc.
        PO Box 1162
        Minnetonka, MN 55345
        Toll free: 1-877-PEYTRAL (877-739-8725)
        FAX: 952-906-9777
        www.peytral.com

Publisher's Cataloging-in-Publication
(Provided by Quality Books, Inc.)

Moore, Lorraine O.
    Inclusion, strategies for working with young children
    :a resource guide for teachers, childcare providers,
    and parents / Lorraine O. Moore -- 2nd ed.
        p.cm.
    Includes bibliographical references.
    ISBN 1-890455-33-4

    1. Inclusive education--United States--Handbooks,
    manuals, etc. 2. Children with disabilities--Education
    (Early childhood)--United States--Handbooks, manuals,
    etc. I. Title.

        LC1201.M66 2003   371.9'046
                                    QBI02-200888

Table of Contents

Preface...7

Introduction 9

Chapter One..11
Working with Young Children..11
Major Findings from Brain Research..11
"Whole Child" Perspective 13
Developmentally Appropriate Practice...14
Cycles of Learning 15
       Phase I – Awareness 16
       Phase II – Exploration...16
       Phase III – Inquiry 16
       Phase IV – Utilization or Application............................17
Environmental Considerations..18
Testing and Labeling of Young Children 19
Working with Parents..19
Teaching from the Heart 20

Chapter Two 21
Inclusion: The Right to Equal Educational Experiences 21
Children with Special Needs...22
Types of Special Needs...23
Criteria for Labeling...25
Legislation That Supports Inclusive Education...................................26
Inclusion...27
Benefits of Inclusive Education...28
Barriers to Inclusive Education 29
Summary...30

Chapter Three 33
General Strategies for Working with Young Children 33
Expectations...33
Time..34
Environmental Conditions 34
Nutrition and Learning 36
Multi-Sensory Activities 36
Basic Categories of Modification 37
Brain Balancing..37

Chapter Four 39
Communication Strategies 39
Basic Communication Strategies 39
Attending Strategies...40
Listening Strategies...41
Attaching Meaning to Print and Words 42
Strategies for Children with a Hearing Impairment 45
Strategies for Children with a Visual Impairment. 46
Strategies and Information for Children with Limited Speech
and Expressive Language 48

Chapter Five 51
Large and Small Motor Development 51
Strategies for Large Motor Development 51
Strategies for Small Motor Development 53

Chapter Six 57
Emotional/Social Development 57
Strategies for Supporting Emotional Development 58
Strategies for Supporting Social Development 60

Chapter Seven 65
Guiding and Modifying Children's Behavior 65
General Strategies for Guiding Children's Behavior 65
Strategies for Modifying Children's Behavior 68
Strategies for Children with Attention Problems 69
Strategies for Aggressive and Withdrawn Behaviors 72
Strategies for Problem Solving 74

Chapter Eight 77
Preparatory Writing, Reading, and Math Skills...........................77
Preparatory Writing and Reading Strategies 78
Preparatory Math Skills 84

Chapter Nine 87
Assessing Young Children...87
Characteristics of Young Children That Affect Assessment 87
Developmental Patterns..88
Purposes for Assessing Young Children..89
Assessment Tools and Techniques..90
Observation 90
Interviews..91
Standardized Tests..92
Other Assessment Procedures 94
Assessment of Children with Special Needs 94
Summary...96

Chapter Ten 97
The Future of Learning 97
Brain Research 98
Nutrition and Learning 98
Other Needs of the Brain and Body 99
Environmental Factors and Learning..100
Expanded View of Intelligence 100
Responsibility 101

Appendix A 103
Forms and Activities..103
Form 1 - Profile of Development 104
Form 2 - Cycles of Learning 105
**Form 3 - Behavior as a Function of the Interaction of the Child in
         His Environment** 107
Form 4 - General Strategies for Working with Young Children 108
Form 5 - Categories of Modifications...109
Form 6 - Creating a Personal Dictionary of Familiar Objects 112
Form 7 - Mazes...114
Form 8 - Learning about Feelings Through Working with Animals.....116
Form 9 - Sharing and Talking about Feelings......................................118
Form 10 -Learning about Feelings Through Dramatic Play 119
Form 11 -Learning about Empathy 120
Form 12 -Settling Conflicts Peacefully..121
Form 13 -Steps for Problem Solving 123
Form 14 -Steps in Changing Behavior...124
Form 15 -Charting Frequency of Behaviors...125
Form 16 -Child Observation Form 127
Form 17 -Examples of Observation Forms 130
Form 18 -Interview about the Child..134

Appendix B 136
Bibliography 136

Appendix C 139
Resources 139

Appendix D 140
Glossary 140

Preface

My interest in writing this book was inspired by the many insightful children I have worked with as a teacher and psychologist over the past years. I have shared their joy and excitement, their hopes, their disappointments, their struggles with learning, and their attempts to survive in an often harsh world. My love for children, the gratitude I have for all that they have taught me, and my desire to help create a better place in which children can learn and grow have inspired me to write this book. It is to these children, to my children John and Jane, and to all children everywhere that I dedicate this book.

There have been many adults who deeply inspired me along my journey of working with children. It is because of their love, caring, and support that I am able to continue my work for the benefit of children. I especially want to acknowledge and thank Roberto and Peggy Hammeken (Peytral Publications) for their encouragement and continued support in the publication of this book and of my previous book *Inclusion: A Practical Guide for Parents*.

Jennet Grover's expertise in editing and commitment to making this a quality book for all who read it is greatly appreciated.

This Space is for your notes

Introduction

Young children need to experience an environment within which they are loved and supported for who they are. They need peers of similar age with which to interact socially and to grow emotionally, so they can successfully proceed through necessary developmental stages. Inclusion, the practice of providing programs that include children with and without special needs in the same setting, offers the best opportunity for healthy social growth and for proper sequential development of learning skills.

This book was written for the purpose of helping adults who work with 3-to7- year old children in school programs, early childhood settings (including preschools and day care programs), home-based programs, and Head Start programs.

Contained in this book are both guidelines and strategies for adults working with this age group. These can also be used for young children who are developmentally more advanced than the average child, and for older children who are developmentally delayed in one or more areas.

The first chapter of this book outlines some *child-focused* rather than *curriculum-focused* guidelines for working with young children. The guidelines and strategies can be used as they are written or can be adapted to fit the individual needs of the child and his setting.

The second chapter provides an overview and discussion of what inclusion is and the categories of special needs and disabilities that are used with children. The remaining chapters include over 350 strategies for working with young children which cover the areas of communication, large and small motor development, emotional/social development, behavioral issues, preparatory writing, reading skills, math skills, and assessment. Sample forms that support the text are included for teachers and other adults working with young children. We encourage you to reproduce these and use them as needed.

Specific reference books on a variety of topics have been recommended for developing or enlarging your resource library and expanding your awareness about working with young children.

After considerable thought, a decision was made to use the generic pronoun "he," as it complies with standard literary practice, instead of using both "he" and "she" which can become very cumbersome for the reader. Unfortunately, until the literary community devises a neutral-gender alternative, we find ourselves in a position to take the more traditional approach for the sake of clarity and simplicity.

This book has been written with a great deal of love and compassion for children of all ages, and in recognition of all the special love and support given by the many adults who provide services for and work with young children. Through the special efforts of parents and other significant adults in children's lives, a difference is made in the future of all children.

Chapter One

Working with Young Children

Children are our future. Being in a position to work with children and guide them through the maze of learning experiences is both a special privilege and a challenge. Success in meeting this challenge is dependent upon our love for children, our understanding of them, and the knowledge we have regarding the planning and implementation of activities that encourage their growth and development.

An explosion of information has emerged from the decade of the 1990's. As a result, we now know how better to support the development and learning of children. Throughout this book you will find concrete ways to put into practice the necessary elements to enhance the growth and development of children by meeting their learning needs in all areas of development. To lay the foundation for putting strategies for working with young children into operation, the first part of this chapter presents a summary of the major findings to emerge from the Decade of the Brain (1990's). The second part of this chapter is devoted to child development concepts that have stood the test of time and resonate with the findings from brain research.

Major Findings from Brain Research

Scientists have come to the point of agreement that both nature and nurture play a significant role in a child's development. At this time there is a general consensus that each accounts for about 50% of who a child becomes. There is an acknowledgement that everyone comes into the world with a genetic inheritance. However, it is the environment that provides the stimuli for an individual's growth and development relative to intelligence, talents, and social abilities. The nature/nurture equation is significant information to pay attention to for all parents and adults who are responsible for a child's welfare and learning. What children come into the world with, plus the type and amount of environmental

stimulation, accounts for each child's growth and development. It is a dynamic interaction of the two represented by the following equation: Behavior (learning, social, etc.) is a function of the person and the environment, $Bf = C + E$. This dynamic interaction makes it imperative that we always consider both factors when providing learning experiences for children and in planning strategies to change their behavior. The power and influence of environmental stimulation and experiences gives encouragement to adults for helping children reach their potential. It is critical that parents of young children, childcare providers, and educators understand what this means and apply it to all environments where children live, play, and learn. Creating these environments is a wonderful opportunity to help children develop their potential. At the same time, it is a major responsibility to provide the environments that will support each child's growth and development. To be most effective, the timing of different types and amounts of stimuli should coincide with the child's readiness to receive it.

Children come into the world with a full set of (about 100 billion) brain cells (neurons). Stimuli from the environment are mandatory for these neurons to grow, develop, and form pathways of communication. These pathways are necessary to provide the means for language development, visual abilities, motor functions, and social/emotional growth to take place. The foundations for the development of these mind/body functions begin during the pre-natal period. Then, from birth up to the first five to six years of a child's life is a critical time for the brain's neural pathways to be hardwired. Future learning and behavior are dependent upon the communications between the neurons in the brain and the cells throughout the body that are established during these early years. Young children need experiences and nurturance from adults to accomplish this important task. The richer the environment, the greater the number of interconnections are made. Consequently, learning can take place faster and with greater meaning.

In being and working with children, it is necessary to approach all we do from a mind/body/heart approach. Neuroscientists and other researchers devoted to studying the physiology of the mind/body/heart have established the fact that these three components are interconnected and work in concert with each other. What we eat effects how we think and feel. What we think and feel affects our body's functions. In other words, cognition, emotion, and physiology are all intertwined. What we do for or to our body directly affects our ability to reason and to maintain a state of emotional balance. What happens to children (and adults) emotionally either enhances or compromises thinking ability and body functions. The body, brain, and emotions contribute to each other in complex and interdependent ways. Knowing this dynamic interplay can help adults to become more aware of ways to provide conditions and experiences that contribute to a balanced state of being, rather than the less productive state of imbalance.

Until recently, emotions were viewed from a psychological perspective consisting of both mental and feeling processes. As scientists became more adept at measuring the effect of emotions on body functions and reasoning abilities, emotions as a study moved into the circle of topics worthy of scientific enquiry. For example, scientists conducting research at the Institute of HeartMath in Boulder Creek, California, have measured the power of emotions by tuning in to heart frequencies and variability rates. They have found that the heart and the brain are constantly communicating with each other via the pathways of the nervous system to connect our thoughts, emotions, and body systems. Emotions, the physiological response of the body to external stimuli, are activated when one or more of our five senses take in information from the environment. This information is then evaluated by the brain's feeling and thinking systems to determine which response is needed. The response can vary from joy and excitement to anger and despair which, in turn, affects our cognitive and body functions either in a positive, neutral, or negative way.

Through scientific research, nutrition has been found to have a direct link to learning and behavior. A balanced diet containing all the necessary nutrients for the brain and body support learning and appropriate behavior. A diet lacking in these nutrients has been linked to poor attention, learning difficulties in academic subjects, and behaviors associated with hyperactivity, aggression, and depression. There has been an increase in national concern about the health of our nation's children as obesity rates and the onset of adult Type II diabetes have increased among today's children. Behavioral problems have also been on the increase, as observed by the increased numbers of children of all ages on some type of medication, extending down to children as young as three years old. A study of a group in San Francisco estimated that as many as 1/3 of our children experience some degree of depression. One of the more promising alternatives to medication has been to treat children by natural means such as through diet. Since nutrition is now accepted as a science, more researchers are committing their time and resources to carrying this endeavor further in order to expand our knowledge of the relationship between nutrition and learning and nutrition and behavior.

Brain/body/heart research has provided us with a substantial body of updated information to help us understand and work with children more effectively. This gives practitioners a scientific basis for evaluating current child development practices to determine which practices to keep and which to change or discard. The ideas and strategies expressed in the remaining pages of this chapter and throughout the book are consistent with the mind/body/heart research.

"Whole Child" Perspective

Children need to be viewed from a "whole child" perspective in order to encourage and ensure a balance in their growth and development. It is the responsibility of adults to be aware of and to address the physical, emotional, cognitive, and spiritual needs of each child. If one area is over-emphasized relative to other areas, children will not obtain the balance they need to develop as "whole people." Balance is critical for children to attain their full potential in all realms of life.

Addressing the needs of the whole child in a learning environment gives children the opportunity to optimize talents as they surface and to address their individual needs, which may be expressed as limitations. This becomes significant for children who experience difficulty in the learning process.

How children feel about themselves is based both upon the love and understanding they receive and upon their performance. Children with learning difficulties need to be encouraged and supported in the processes of discovering their talents and learning to use them. This allows them to develop positive feelings about themselves as people. The possibility of young children imposing the stigma of their learning difficulties universally on all areas of their lives without recognizing their talents in other areas is something that

educators and parents need to recognize and prevent in order to avoid the establishment of permanently formed negative patterning.

Developmentally Appropriate Practice

Everything we plan and do with children needs to be based on the concept referred to as *developmentally appropriate practice*. This concept is based on two principal ideas. The first idea conveys the fact that all practices in working with children need to reflect realistic expectations for children typical of their age group. The second idea refers to the fact that practices in working with children should also be individually appropriate. Practices that are both age appropriate and individually appropriate provide the greatest opportunity for children to develop and learn at a pace that will maximize their progress.

Development and learning are interdependent. This relationship can be implemented for each child by planning and delivering instruction and materials that fall within a child's zone of proximal development, a concept developed by Vygotsky. According to Vygotsky, a child's place of instruction and progress is determined by knowing where a child is when placed on a continuum of mastery from "can do independently" to "cannot do." Visually, this continuum appears as:

Zone of Proximal Development

child does alone	*child does with assistance*	*child cannot do*

Figure 1

A child's placement on this continuum is based on observation of the child's spontaneous behaviors and the child's assisted behaviors. Informal and formal testing can supplement the observations made by the adults working with a specific child. The zone of proximal development for a particular child lies between what the child can do with minimal assistance and what the child can do with maximum assistance in a supportive environment. Possible supports include interaction with the teacher, another child, or equipment and materials. All children can do more than they can manage alone, but the direction of growth, development, and learning is toward independence.

Another important aspect of linking learning to development is not to only be aware of where a child is in his *overall* development, but also where the child is in *each area* of development. This includes assessing where a child's language, motor, visual-motor integration, cognitive, social/emotional abilities, etc., lie on the developmental continuum.

It is important to remember that a profile depicting an uneven development of abilities is not uncommon for young children. This is certainly true for children with special needs where, in some instances, a child may be within an average range of development in one or more areas, but be significantly delayed in others.

Using the Gesell Institute's guideline of (+/-) 6 months of a child's chronological age as representing development within a normal range of expectation, profiles of even and uneven development appear in Figure 2.

Profiles of Development

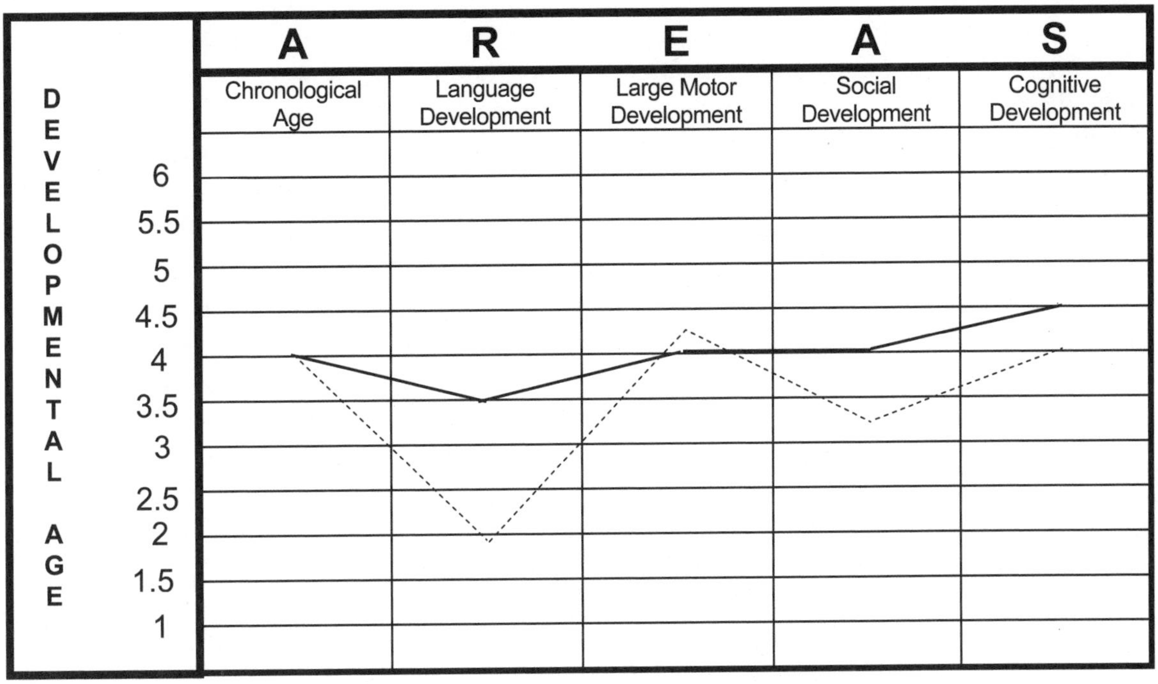

		A	R	E	A	S
D E V E L O P M E N T A L A G E		Chronological Age	Language Development	Large Motor Development	Social Development	Cognitive Development
	6					
	5.5					
	5					
	4.5					
	4					
	3.5					
	3					
	2.5					
	2					
	1.5					
	1					

Key: ——————— *A four year old boy with all areas of development within (+/-) 6 months of his chronological age*

-------------- *A four-year-old boy with a severe language delay*

Figure 2

Refer to Form 1 in Appendix A for a Profile of Development you can use to chart a child's development.

Cycles of Learning

The concept of Cycles of Learning, as endorsed by the National Association for the Education of Young Children and the National Association of Early Childhood Specialists in State Departments of Education, provides a foundation for learning experiences for children. According to this concept, any new learning by children (or adults) follows a relatively predictable pattern or cycle. Cycles of Learning is based on the assumption that a child's learning reflects a four-phase, recurring cycle that begins in awareness, moves to exploration, then to inquiry, and, finally, to utilization.

Phase I - Awareness

In this first cycle of learning, children begin to acquire knowledge through experiencing events, objects, people, or ideas in their environment. As they process these various experiences, they develop an interest in what they see and begin to recognize some broad parameters which they will explore in the next phase of the learning cycle.

It is the responsibility of adults to create environments for engaging children's interest by introducing them to new objects, events, and people on a regular basis. During this phase, it is important that teachers and other adults feed a child's interest by posing problems or questions, by responding to a child's curiosity or shared experience, and by displaying enthusiasm. These conditions will then give the child the impetus to move on to the next phase in the cycle of learning, that of **exploration.**

Phase II - Exploration

Exploration is the process whereby children activate all of their senses to evaluate the components or attributes of the events, objects, and people brought into their awareness in Phase I.

It is important that children construct their own personal meaning of their experiences during this time. Teachers can facilitate this by providing opportunities for active exploration, by supporting and enhancing exploration by asking open-ended questions, by respecting the child's thinking and rule systems, and by allowing for errors.

When the child has attached personal meaning to the experience and begins to draw conclusions about his experiences, it is time to move on to the third phase in the cycle of learning, that of **inquiry**. It is important to note that even though this may appear to be a linear process, in reality, children can be simultaneously engaged in two or more phases at the same time.

Phase III - Inquiry

Awareness and exploration are essential but insufficient for complete understanding. A child's personal interpretations and conclusions will contain limitations imposed by the child's lack of experience and knowledge. Adults must correct and expand this thinking within the context of the child's subculture and his society. Inquiry is the process whereby children can analyze and compare their own behaviors and conclusions with what is generally accepted in a context that takes into account their developmental level.

It is the teacher's responsibility during this time to help children refine their understanding through focusing their attention, asking questions, and providing information links and other support necessary for increasing the children's understanding. The realizations and knowledge gained by children during this next phase need to be brought to the application level to fully personalize the learning and make it useful.

Phase IV - Utilization or Application

This is the functional level of learning, the stage where children can apply or make use of the learning they have acquired through the experiencing of events, objects, people, or concepts. It is at this point that the learning acquires value. It is also a point at which the learning cycle repeats itself due to the new awareness that emerges from the utilization of knowledge and understanding. As children focus on applying their learning, it becomes the teacher's responsibility to create ways for children to apply this new knowledge and understanding in a variety of situations.

To illustrate this cycle, think of the process of introducing color to children through the use of watercolor paints to create a pattern or a picture.

1. ***Awareness Phase***: The teacher introduces the children to the idea of exploring color through watercolor paints, by having the necessary materials set out for the children to see and having some watercolor pictures placed around the room.

2. ***Exploration Phase***: The teacher encourages the children to look at the materials and pictures. Given minimal directions, children then explore the concept of color by first working with one color and then progressing to mixing two or more colors together. As the children explore color through this means, they make observations about what happens when they combine colors, how the various colors make them feel, and how the colors look.

3. ***Inquiry Phase***: Children's observations are shared with each other. One conclusion reached is that if you mix several colors together, you get brown. At this point the teacher encourages children to share other things they have learned about color and which colors make them feel the best. It is the teacher's responsibility to clear up any incorrect conclusions and extend the children's knowledge about color appropriate for their age group.

4. ***Utilization or Application Phase:*** The focus for this phase is on the functional use of what the children have learned about the various colors: what happens when you mix certain colors together, how each color or combination of colors makes you feel, etc. For younger children, let them think about ways in which this information can be used in their everyday lives, such as the application of color in the clothes they wear and the foods they eat, how color is used in their homes, etc.

Application of this framework can be applied to the process of learning to read, learning to write, learning mathematics, and learning any other subject matter or concept. All educators are encouraged to think about this conceptual framework in their daily work with children and to use it as a tool for analyzing and planning appropriate curricula for individuals and groups of children.

See Form 2 in Appendix A for an expansion of the format for using this approach with children.

Environmental Considerations

The behaviors we observe and record are a result of the inner child interacting with the environmental elements of people, animals, plants, inanimate objects, and of the conditions surrounding the child's interaction. Figure 3 below depicts this idea visually.

Child/Environment Interaction

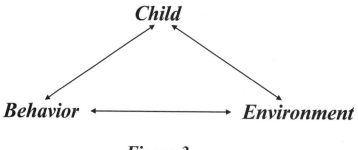

Figure 3

Behaviors (including learning behaviors) require that we pay attention to the child *and the environment* in which the learning takes place. As represented by this model, it is assumed that behavior, child, and environment are mutually and reciprocally influential. The implication of this model for meeting the needs of young children in all aspects of their development requires that we pay closer attention to the quality of children's interactions with other children and with adults in all environments, and to all conditions in which these interactions take place. This model can be used to help understand children's behaviors, to determine where potential problems exist, and to plan appropriate interventions for children having difficulty in learning and/or behavior.

The next few paragraphs will address some environmental conditions considered significant when working with young children. Comments will be restricted to physical aspects of events and space that impact children in the environments in which learning and childcare programs take place.

Events: Recognizing that children participate in several environments (such as home, neighborhood, school/daycare, community, etc.), it is important to have a sense of what each of these environments is like for a particular child. For example, it is generally understood that a child carries what is going on at home wherever he goes. If the child carries love, peace, and a feeling of belonging, this will be reflected in the attitudes and feelings he carries into other situations and environments. With a positive home atmosphere, the child is better able to participate and learn in the school or daycare environment.

Similarly, if a child experiences conflict, trauma, continual transition, or economic hardship, he carries the burden and impact of these events and is less likely to reach out to others and participate to his full potential in other environments. When this situation exists, the teacher or childcare worker needs to play a much more significant role in the child's life in order to give him love, security, and a sense of belonging, necessary ingredients for success in learning.

Physical Space: The impact of lighting, color, sound, and organization of physical space on children's behavior and learning ability has been researched and is emerging as a contributing factor in a child's success or lack of success in the learning process. Adults responsible for designing and implementing programs for children need to address and apply this research.

Refer to Form 3 in Appendix A for more information on this topic.

Testing and Labeling of Young Children

A basic premise to remember in testing young children is that *the younger the child, the less reliable the testing results.* This is due to several factors. First is the fact that formal tests are often based on small samples (few items) of testing behaviors. Second, the difficulty inherent in testing children due to their minimal attention span must be addressed. Third, young children may have difficulty meeting the structural demands of testing, such as being unable to understand instructions, being unable to sit still for extended periods of time, etc. Fourth, during this growth period, young children are changing at a rapid rate, which means they are always in transition.

Due to the above conditions in the testing of young children, the labeling of various handicapping conditions needs to be done with a great deal of caution. Labeling of young children is further complicated by the fact that it is difficult to distinguish between difficulties related to developmental rate and difficulties related to organic causes. This is especially true for children who display only mild difficulties when compared to the expectations for similar age peers.

To chart a young child's progress adequately and to determine his ongoing needs, it is necessary to conduct testing more frequently than for older children. Also, a variety of tests should be used in assessing young children, including formal (standardized) tests, informal (created by the teacher) tests, observations, and parental information.

Working with Parents

Children are more successful in the learning process when educators and parents work together for the benefit of the child in a school or daycare setting. Meeting the needs of the whole child, especially those with disabilities, in a regular setting challenges our creativity for adapting curricula, developing appropriate teaching strategies, and structuring the learning environment. Success in meeting this challenge requires joint cooperation of parents and educators on a continual basis.

Teaching from the Heart

Children are very perceptive about how adults feel toward them. They are able to discern the difference if we tell them that we love them, but do not ultimately demonstrate this love through our body language or gestures. They connect with adults through feeling rather than through the spoken word. In working with young children, it is therefore imperative that we connect with them at the heart level, allowing our teaching and interactions with them to come from the heart first and, secondly, from the knowledge from our minds.

Recent research conducted at the Institute of HeartMath in Boulder Creek, California, has led to the discovery that the heart is vital to effective learning on all levels - mentally, physically, and emotionally. Generating feelings of love, caring, appreciation, and compassion towards young children helps reach children at the heart level to enhance their learning. These behaviors encourage children to feel, learn, and extend these behaviors to other children and adults.

When adults come from a place of love, children have a greater opportunity to self-generate feelings of love, caring, appreciation, and compassion. This, according to the research, enhances intuitive perception and increases coherence and clarity in children.

Approximately 40% of the heart's function is that of being a pump. The other major function of the heart is that of being a balancing organ that acts as an input system to the brain. This contributes to a child's emotional balance, which plays a significant role in learning and adapting to the demands of any given situation.

It is imperative that adults who work with young children understand the significance of the relationship of teaching from the heart (expressed as love and compassion) to the growth and development of children. Love, given unconditionally, is the most powerful educational tool we have. Heart intelligence, as a contributor to children's learning, is an exciting new frontier of knowledge to be explored for the benefit of all children and adults alike.

Chapter Two

Inclusion:
The Right to Equal
Educational Experiences

All children have both similar and unique characteristics. For children who have special needs, it is important to remember first that all children have similar needs. These include the physical needs for shelter, rest, and nourishment, as well as the psychological needs to be nurtured, safe, and accepted. Second, children with developmental delays and disabilities have needs that are not shared by all other children. They need environments that are specifically organized and adjusted to minimize the effects of their disabilities and to promote their growth and development through the learning process.

In the past, it was felt that children with special needs could best be nurtured and serviced in environments separate from children without special needs. Currently, there is a major movement across the United States toward including children with special needs in the same environments that service children without special needs. Experience and research have been the impetus, resulting in legislation to make this a reality. Concern for the rights of each individual to have equal access to all facilities and services led to the passage of the Americans with Disabilities Act (P.L. 101-336) in 1990. Full implementation of this act (the ADA) in conjunction with the Individuals with Disabilities Education Act (formerly known as the Education of the Handicapped Act) requires that all early childhood programs as well as school programs be prepared to serve children with special needs.

This chapter will focus on the implications of this mandate for all early childhood educators in the designing and implementation of early childhood programs. Special needs, as they apply to young children, will be addressed first.

Children with Special Needs

The term "special needs," in the context of this book, is used to describe children with disabilities or developmental delays. Young children are considered to have special needs when their well-being, development, and learning are compromised if special attention is not given during their early education. This attention can best be provided by knowledgeable educators and childcare providers who work with these children and their families in early childhood centers and school programs.

In the past, children with special needs have been referred to as *exceptional* children, *handicapped* children, *special education* children, etc. These terms should no longer be used to refer to this group of children, as it calls attention to their disabilities, negating the fact that they are children first and foremost. It is only after recognizing their qualities as children that their disabilities should be noted. If the focus is on the disability, which implies limitation, their gifts and development as *whole people* can too easily be ignored.

Children with disabilities are generally classified by a system that defines criteria of eligibility for early intervention and special education services. To be eligible for such services under the Individuals with Disabilities Act (IDEA-formerly the Education of the Handicapped Act), children can fit into any of the categories listed below:

- Specific learning disability
- Speech (language) impairment
- Serious emotional disturbance
- Visual impairment and blindness
- Hearing impairment and deafness
- Mental retardation
- Multiple handicaps
- Orthopedic impairment
- Other health impairment
- Traumatic brain injury
- Autism

Because of the difficulty in detecting mild forms of disability in young children and the detrimental effects of early labeling, IDEA allows states to use the category of "developmental delay" for young children with special needs. To make this category operational, each state has specific criteria and measurement procedures for determining children's eligibility for early intervention and special education services. What constitutes a developmental delay is also included in each state's guidelines. To truly honor children, to respect the development of the whole child, and to acknowledge the tenuousness of assessing and labeling young children, it is in the best interests of all children to initially use the label of developmental delay whenever the full manifestation of a disability is not readily demonstrated.

Types of Special Needs

Some children will be diagnosed by their physician as having specific conditions and/or syndromes which may meet eligibility for special services. Examples of these diagnoses include cerebral palsy, spina bifida, muscular dystrophy, and Down Syndrome. It is also important to keep in mind that children exposed to cocaine, alcohol, or other dangerous substances in utero can be affected developmentally. However, the impact of these exposures can be difficult to detect at birth; they usually surface when a child reaches early childhood or school age. For purposes of understanding the various categories of special needs when working with young children, it is helpful to group them as follows:

Developmental Delay: According to the Individuals with Disabilities Act, states may use this classification for young children with special needs. Each state makes its own determination as to what constitutes a developmental delay and what criteria are used to determine eligibility. Generally, to be eligible for special education services, a child needs to be significantly delayed, relative to his peer group, in one or more areas of development.

Speech/Language Impairment: A speech disorder exists when a child has a difficult time correctly reproducing spoken sounds and words, smoothly producing words in sequence, and/or producing sounds and words equivalent to other children of similar age. When diagnosing young children's speech sounds, it is imperative to use the developmental age reference points for the development of each of the speech sounds.

A language disability exists when a child has difficulty expressing needs, ideas, or information compared to age expectation. This situation is often accompanied by problems in understanding language as well as the verbal expression of language. These children often get frustrated when they need to express themselves verbally, as they often know more than they can say in words. Cueing into gestures and other non-verbal behaviors is extremely important in understanding and working with these children.

Hearing Impairment: Most children with hearing impairments are classified as hard-of-hearing rather than having a total loss of hearing. Children who have a hard-of-hearing diagnosis cannot hear the spoken word clearly, but this can often be improved with hearing aids. A young child's social behaviors and performance is almost always affected by a hearing impairment. These children need extra visual input and demonstrations to show them how to engage in and accomplish given tasks compared to the average child their age.

Visual Impairment: A child who is totally blind must depend on his non-visual senses, primarily hearing and touch, to access information. A child with even a partial visual handicap has an impairment that means, even with correction, the child's every day performance on visually dependent tasks will be compromised. A child with partial sight has a limited ability to see print, other objects, and movement, even with lenses. All written materials and visual tasks need to be adapted to accommodate these children. Since their senses other than sight tend to be more highly developed, encouraging the use of these other

senses should be incorporated into these children's programs to improve their success in learning.

Mental Impairment:
Children with this disability have significantly lower intelligence for learning verbal and non-verbal symbols involved in learning compared to similarly aged peers. In young children, this is often demonstrated by a slower rate of learning the skills associated with expectations for their chronological age and may appear as a developmental delay in cognitive abilities. This disability becomes more apparent as children engage in academic skills.

Emotional/Behavioral Disorder:
A child with this disorder shows behavioral and emotional responses in a preschool or school setting that is significantly different from, and inappropriate compared to those of similarly aged peers. These behaviors or emotional responses, in turn, interfere to a significant extent with the child's social interactions and learning and/or the learning of other children. Children with this disorder often need counseling in addition to specific structures and expectations set up in the school environment.

Pervasive Developmental Disorder (PDD):
This disorder is characterized by severe and pervasive impairments in several areas of development. This includes the areas of communication skills, social interaction skills, and/or the presence of stereotyped repetitive behaviors, interests, and activities. This disorder is usually evident in the first few years of a child's life. Some degree of mental retardation is often associated with PDD. Children who have this disorder generally need a considerable number of modifications in their instructional programs, activities, and expectations if they are to achieve success.

Autism:
Autism is a developmental disability that occurs during infancy or early childhood. It is a behaviorally defined syndrome characterized by an uneven developmental profile. Most children with this diagnosis demonstrate qualitative impairments in reciprocal social interactions and with verbal and non-verbal communication. These children also tend to have a markedly restricted repertoire of interests and activities.

Repetitive, obsessive behaviors and sensory overload are problems also associated with autism.

Autism is a spectrum disorder that includes mild to severe forms of associated behaviors. The mild form of autism is usually referred to as Asperger's Syndrome. However, the DSM-IV classifies Asperger's Syndrome as a separate disorder. Controversy currently exists as to whether Asperger's is a distinct syndrome or a form of autism.

Traumatic Brain Injury:
This term applies to open or closed head injuries caused by an external force rather than to brain injuries that are congenital or degenerative conditions or brain injuries induced by birth trauma. This type of diagnosis is made if a child's learning and/or social interactions are impacted to a degree of severity to warrant the need for special education and related services.

Specific Learning Disability: A specific learning disability is a disorder in which a child's learning performance and achievement are significantly below his measured ability or potential for academic learning. A specific learning disability interferes with a child's ability to acquire, organize, and/or express information relevant to school functioning when given only the normal developmental opportunities and instruction provided in a regular school environment.

The discrepancy between a child's performance and achievement compared to his potential is generally due to an information-processing difficulty. This can occur at the input, integration, and/or output levels of information processing; it is not due to environmental and/or biological factors.

Physical Impairment: A child with this disorder has a physical impairment that often adversely affects the child's educational performance. Examples of this disability include cerebral palsy, spina bifida, and muscular dystrophy. Physical impairments play out differently for each child in terms of ability to learn and participate in the regular education program. If difficulties occur, individualized plans and accommodations are often needed to facilitate a child's success.

Other Health Impairment: This diagnosis refers to children who have limited strength, vitality, or alertness due to chronic or acute health problems, such as heart conditions, asthma, epilepsy, cancer, diabetes, Acquired Immune Deficiency Syndrome (AIDS), etc. These conditions generally result in absenteeism from school, which interferes with the child's learning progress. Special programs and schedules often need to be set up between the home and school so that these children can establish continuity in their learning.

Criteria for Labeling

Labeling of young children is primarily for the purpose of determining eligibility for receiving special education services under federal and state guidelines. It is by no means intended as a structure for curriculum and instructional purposes. Children who share the same label have a diversity of needs based on the degree of severity (from mild to profound) of their disability and the way in which their disability impacts learning and social interactions. Curriculum and instruction should therefore be based on each child's individual needs and skill development relative to how he functions in his environments.

In addition to the conditions inherent when assessing and diagnosing young children, there are two different criteria used by the various states for program placement. Some states use a percentage discrepancy formula that ranges from 25% to 50% for eligibility and placement purposes. Other states use standard-deviation ranges from 1.5 to 2.0 as a discrepancy ratio. This means that a child may qualify for services in one state but may not qualify in another state.

To complicate matters further, states vary in their definitions and criteria for eligibility for special education services based on what they feel is a developmental delay. The label of developmental delay is utilized by many states until these children reach the age

of six or seven. At this age, this label is often changed to a specific category, such as learning disability, if a child continues to demonstrate a need for special education services.

Legislation That Supports Inclusive Education

The model most often supported by recent legislation, and supported by experience and research for servicing children with special needs is inclusive education. Inclusive education, commonly referred to as *inclusion* is defined as teaching children with special needs in the same environments as children without special needs. Inclusion allows for the needs of children with and without disabilities to be met in the same programs. This requires that the special education teacher and/or consultant goes to the child in the normal school setting, rather than the child going to the special education teacher in a setting separate from other children.

There are a number of major laws regarding the concept of inclusion which have influenced the current status of special education for children from age three through age twenty-one who have disabilities.

Handicapped Children's Early Education - P.L. 90-538 (1968) (currently known as the Early Education Program for Children with Disabilities).

This law authorizes funds for the development, evaluation, and dissemination of model programs for serving infants and young children with disabilities. This law and the action resulting from it gave birth to the concept of early childhood special education.

Education for All Handicapped Children - P.L. 94-142 (1975).

This law established a national policy related to the education of children from ages three through age twenty-one with disabilities. However, the major impact of this law was for children six years of age and older. In spite of this fact, its provisions have been central in shaping current early childhood special education. For example, it was at this point that an Individualized Education Program (plan) for all children with special needs was established.

Amendment to the Education for All Handicapped Children - P.L. 99-457.

The amendments to this law reauthorize EHA (P.L. 94-142 see above) and mandate early intervention services for infants and young children who are developmentally disabled or at risk for disabilities. This law forms the basis of our current practices for preschool children with special needs.

Individuals with Disabilities - P.L. 101-576 (1990).

This law reauthorized the Education for All Handicapped Children Act and renamed it the Individuals with Disabilities Education Act. The categories of autism and traumatic brain injury were added as recognized disabilities. IDEA was updated in 1997 and is currently referenced as PL105-17. This act is up for renewal in 2002.

Americans with Disabilities - P.L. 101-336 (1990).

As major civil rights legislation, this law extends beyond education. It requires that individuals with disabilities have equal access to public and private services, including equal access to enrollment in early childhood facilities.

These laws and their subsequent amendments have become the foundation for children from birth to age twenty-one with special needs. It was reported by the U.S. Department of Education that all states had mandates in effect to provide free, appropriate education to preschoolers (children three through five years of age) beginning with the 1992-1993 school year. According to Worley et al, 1993, the majority of early childhood programs of various types reported enrolling at least one child with a developmental delay or disability in 1993.

The implication of these laws and state mandates is that all preschool programs and early childhood educational programs need to be prepared to admit one or more children with special needs. If preschool and other early childhood programs and school settings for all children are to use a model founded on the philosophy of inclusion as the best way to service children with special needs, a thorough understanding of this model is necessary. The remainder of this chapter will be devoted to this understanding.

Inclusion

The inclusion model for educating children with special needs looks like this:

Model of Inclusion

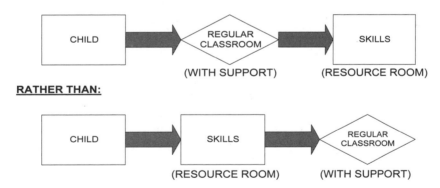

Figure 4

This model of inclusion moves away from a dualistic system of serving children with special needs which has been prevalent in public schools in the past. Implementation of the inclusion model will decrease the use of "separate settings" (buildings or rooms) as places where children with special needs will be given the services they need. Instead, they will receive all or most of their services in a heterogeneous setting, even though the goals for a particular child are different from those of their peers. The philosophy and practice of

inclusion requires that educational systems adapt to the child rather than the child needing to adapt to the system. It is a child-focused approach to education that is clearly supported by legislation and upheld by recent court decisions.

From a practical standpoint, it is important to note that the model of inclusion displayed in Figure 4 is based on a continuum of special education services. Recognition is first given to the rights of children with special needs to have full access to the same settings and programs as children without special needs. Secondly, they have a right to receive special education in these settings. Thirdly, if all attempts to meet a child's needs in an inclusive setting do not result in success relative to an individual's learning goals, a child still has the right to more intense and differentiated services in a setting apart from his peers. This third option may need to surface for some children with severe or profound degrees of disability.

Providing a continuum of special education services conflicts with the choice made by some school districts, which have moved toward a full inclusion model. In this model, all children with disabilities receive their special education services within the regular preschool or educational setting only. For either of these forms of inclusion to be successful in meeting the needs of young children with disabilities, an emergence of educators and special education teachers working together for the benefit of all children must take place.

Children with special needs, when placed in inclusive settings, will need modifications, adaptations, and support, just as they would if they were in a separate setting. However, the delivery system for providing these elements is different. In this instance, support is provided by a special education teacher who consults with the early childhood teacher, and/or a paraprofessional or special education teacher who works as a team member in the classroom. This delivery system requires that there be collaboration between professionals and parents to provide the most appropriate experiences for young children.

Benefits of Inclusive Education

What are the benefits of this delivery system referred to as inclusive education? There are many benefits for young children when they receive an inclusive education rather than a "separate" education. These have been documented from the experiences of educators and parents as well as from research that has been conducted over the past few years.

One of the primary benefits found for young children in inclusive settings is the increased growth in their social skills as a result of their socializing with similar age peers. From their observation and interaction with peers, they experience social behaviors appropriate for their age. This experience allows them to internalize these behaviors and demonstrate them to a greater degree than possible in "separate" settings.

Inclusive education promotes a better sense of belonging, a basic human need, according to Abraham Maslow's theory of psychology. Maslow pointed out that belonging is an essential and prerequisite human need that has to be met before one is able to achieve a sense of self-worth.

For some children, a degree of this sense of self-worth can come from achievement. For children who have difficulty learning and performing, it becomes critical that this sense of belonging provides the basis for self-worth. In turn, a positive self-worth provides the motivation for a child to put forth more effort into his learning. Belonging also has implications for a child's future performance in society.

Inclusive education allows a child to exercise his basic right to be educated with his peers. It emphasizes an unconditional acceptance of each child as a child, without undue focus put on his limitations. With inclusion, the child has the opportunity to participate in all facets of an early childhood or school setting rather than being fragmented into discrete parts based on needs that arise from his limitations. This provides a holistic approach to learning and a better assurance of keeping the needs of the whole child in balance.

Inclusive education minimizes the effects of labeling for the young child. This is an important benefit, as it allows greater flexibility in adjusting to the impact of maturation and development on a child's performance.

A more realistic community experience for a child with special needs is provided through inclusive settings. Through this experience, children can gain better adaptive skills. They can have more opportunities to develop friendships with normally developing peers.

Inclusive education is also beneficial for children without disabilities. It gives these children an opportunity to learn about others who are different from them, while providing them with a better representation of society as it is normally experienced.

Parents who have children both with and without disabilities have reported positive feelings about inclusion. The benefits derived from the modifications and adaptations made in inclusive settings can be used for all children to facilitate the learning process.

Communication between early childhood staff, school staff, and special education staff is increased through the practice of inclusion. Through this communication, special education staff develops a better understanding of classroom content and the typical development of children, whereas general education teachers develop a better understanding of the needs of children with disabilities.

Both groups of staff develop better ways to modify content for young children and develop reasonable expectations across all areas of learning where needed for particular children. Working together, they can also develop more efficient and effective strategies for children to use in acquiring skills. The combined expertise and resources of general education with special education programs and services maximize the learning benefits for all children.

Barriers to Inclusive Education

A common response to change, on the part of many human beings is to resist moving into the unknown. This human trait is a barrier to the restructuring of the philosophy and belief systems which can provide appropriate learning experiences and services for young children with special needs.

A philosophical difference still exists among professionals regarding the best model for servicing young children. These differences exist among early childhood and primary grade professionals, early childhood and primary grade special education professionals, and between the two groups.

Training institutions are still predominantly educating the two groups of professionals that provide services for young children as separate groups rather than

integrating common elements of both. This is often further compounded by inadequate training for both groups of professionals in understanding and adapting content and strategies for individual children at their local sites.

Even though inclusion as a model for meeting the needs of children with disabilities has been positive, supported by research, and backed by legislation and court decisions, there is still some reluctance on the part of some educators to move into this new model. This resistance will act as a barrier until the key people delivering services to children move beyond their resistance and commit themselves to trying something different.

Once a commitment to inclusion as a philosophy and practice for the delivery of special education programs and services is made, on-site training for all staff becomes primary for successful implementation. Insufficient staff training presents a detriment to inclusion's effectiveness.

Funding remains a continuing problem for special education services. The appropriation of funds in many instances, at both federal and state levels, has not increased in the same ratio that the need for services has increased.

The whole question of monitoring special education in private settings remains an unresolved issue. Insufficient monitoring and/or inappropriate monitoring of programs can hinder the success of inclusion in any setting.

Summary

The benefits of inclusion will not occur without purposeful and careful support systems to promote them. For example, even though imitation is a natural way for young children to connect with an experience and learn from it, children with disabilities may not engage in this process automatically or successfully with only one event. They may need additional instruction from caring and trained adults. They may also need encouragement to engage in social exchanges to promote their social development and fulfill their socialization needs. Inclusion in and of itself will not guarantee that these benefits will occur.

Even though we have referred to children with special needs as a group for discussion purposes, it is imperative to remember that each child has individual needs that may be very different from a child who has a similar disability by label. The Federal mandate that each child have his own Individual Educational Program in writing is appropriate to ensure that each child receives the support, adaptations, and modifications that will facilitate his growth and development.

Training programs need to be critically evaluated for their effectiveness in preparing professionals to work with young children in the most productive ways. Changes should be implemented as needed.

As more and more preschools, early childhood centers, and public schools are adopting the practice of inclusive schooling, educators and parents are being met with new challenges. To meet these challenges, more creative approaches and collaborative efforts are necessary to meet the learning, social, and emotional needs of children with disabilities. Inclusion provides individualized care to children with special needs, while forcing the learning systems to expand and be creative in order to meet these needs. When this is done, all children will benefit.

Strategies

The remainder of this book will focus on strategies designed to be used with all children, based on the concept that in working with young children, we need to start at a child's functional or developmental level and use strategies that are the most effective for that level.

The strategies listed in the following chapters are meant to act as springboards for the creative generation of additional strategies by the user. Children will be the happy recipients of everyone's efforts.

Chapter Three

General Strategies for Working with Young Children.

Many of the strategies found effective in working with children who do not have special needs can be used with children who do have special needs. These strategies should be tried first in the context of a child's experiential learning.

If and when these strategies are not effective with children having special needs, adaptations of common strategies and the creation of new strategies should emerge. The strategies listed in this chapter represent a generalized approach for working with young children.

Expectations

1. Expectations for the performance of young children need to be based on their developmental/functional skills (what they can do) in specific areas. When a child is having difficulty performing in one or more areas, first evaluate to see if realistic expectations have been set. If not, adjust the expectations to match where the child falls functionally within the zone of proximal development (see Chapter 1) and apply appropriate strategies for that level of functioning.

2. Share the expectations you have for a child with his parents for each area of the child's performance in your setting. If the two sets of expectations are similar, one can assume they are accurate for the child. If not, dialogue with the parents to find the reasons for the discrepancy. Make adjustments in both sets of expectations as needed.

3. Review your expectations for the child on an ongoing basis, as young children often have spurts of growth that will require periodic adjustments of those expectations. Realistic expectations allow the greatest opportunity for young children to be successful in the learning process. Setting expectations at the child's current functional levels is a prerequisite for success in the learning process.

Time

4. Keep in mind that young children with developmental delays or disabilities generally develop at a slower rate than similar age peers in their areas of limitation. However, except in the case of severe disabilities, the sequence of the acquisition of skills is similar for all children. For some children, adjusting this time factor is sufficient; for others, methods of performing the various tasks also need to be adjusted.

5. Children process information at different rates. Children with special needs often need more time to take in information, manipulate it, and respond compared to other children. Allow for this time factor in the amount of work required from the child.

6. Allow the child who processes information more slowly than other children to have extra time between your request for information and the child's response to the question (a seven-second wait time is adequate for most children).

7. Encourage other children to learn to be patient with the child who needs more response time by modeling this behavior when you interact with this type of child. This will afford the child with slower processing time a feeling of acceptance as well as providing encouragement to share his responses.

8. Be aware of a child's peak performance period during the day. Plan for the child to engage in his most difficult activity during this time. If the child is receiving special education services, this may be the best time to schedule these services.

Environmental Conditions

9. As a part of your room arrangement, plan for a space within your room where special education teachers can work with one or more children. This space should be in the most quiet and least trafficked area of the room. Creating such a space not only facilitates cooperation among the professionals of different disciplines but also allows for a space during non-scheduled times or for volunteers and support help to use.

10. Inclusive settings should be structured in such a way as to allow for small-group activity throughout the day, in addition to large-group activity, as appropriate. Children with special needs generally respond better when included in small rather than large groups.

11. Allow a few quiet areas in your room for children who need alone time as part of their day. Let the use of these areas be an option and a privilege for all children.

12. Evaluate your setting to determine the number of spatial alternatives you provide for the children. Ideally, the classroom space would allow for a broad spectrum of activity levels and styles. This includes space for creative movement, places where children can go for privacy, and social spaces for interpersonal interaction, game playing, and group projects. Arrangement and organization of space influences both the learning and behavior of children. Experiment with different arrangements and observe the effect on the children. Make adjustments to bring about an environment that will have the best impact on children's learning and behavior.

13. Become aware of the different background noises within the room and external to it. Work to filter out distracting stimuli by eliminating extraneous sounds if possible. Or, create harmonious environmental sounds through relaxing music, recorded environmental sounds, white noise generators, or even miniature waterfalls. This will be most beneficial for the children who are sensitive to sound and for those who get easily distracted by sound. It will even act as a calmative for some.

14. Note the amount and type of lighting used in your setting. Research suggests this makes a difference in the learning and behavior of children. Full spectrum fluorescent lighting, which contains the color spectrum indicative of natural outdoor light, has been found to support positive learning and behavior better than to cool-white fluorescent lighting. Even though full spectrum lighting is more expensive than regular fluorescent lighting, the cost is justifiable for the benefit of the children who need this consideration.

15. Color can have an influence on the learning and behavior of children. Exposing children to a wide assortment of colors and allowing them to utilize the ones that make them feel calmer and more focused have proved effective in children's performance. In her book *Unicorns Are Real*, Barbara Mesister Vitale elaborates on the successful use of color with children.

16. According to Gloria DeGaetano (*Television and the Lives of Our Children*), "preschoolers are watching more TV than ever, amassing 5,000-6,000 hours of viewing time by age 5." The rapidity of which visual, auditory, and conceptual changes occur on the screen can negatively impact children's sensory systems and sensory-motor integration. This, in turn, can impact their learning. As a teacher or childcare provider, it is important to limit the use of television watching in your setting in order to provide as many three-dimensional experiences as possible compared to the two dimensions of the television screen.

17. Inform parents of the effects of excessive TV watching on children's learning and concentration. Encourage parents to limit their children's TV watching both in hours and in the types of programs they view.

Nutrition and Learning

18. In the past few years, more and more documentation is appearing on the relationship between diet and learning. It has been found that some children do okay with whatever they eat, while others appear to be biochemically vulnerable and reactive to refined carbohydrates, colas, and synthetic substances that go into the body. This can result in restless behaviors, headaches, chronic fatigue, etc. If you observe some of these behaviors in the children you are working with, talk to their parents regarding the diet and eating habits of the child. Suggest appropriate resources if needed.

19. Nutritional deficits (caused by insufficient intake of protein, complex carbohydrates and essential fatty acids) may result in behaviors that are commonly associated with the behaviors of children who have been identified as being hyperactive or as having learning difficulties. Consult with the parents regarding this and refer them to appropriate resources as needed.

20. Talk with your children about the importance of eating healthy foods and explain how foods affect how we feel and learn. Have children document what they eat for a given period of time and then compare their lists with recommended diets.

21. If the children you work with bring snacks or lunches to your setting, encourage them to bring only healthy food.

22. Consult with your school nurse or a nutritionist to gain information sufficient to put together a suggested list of healthy food for children to bring to school.

Multi-Sensory Activities

23. Young children tend to use all of their senses simultaneously. When planning activities for children, incorporate as many of the five senses as you can into each activity.

24. Plan to use movement and the involvement of the child's five senses in your activities whenever possible. This combination provides stimulation to the brain needed to develop the young child's small and large motor coordination, linguistic abilities, and body awareness.

25. For children who have sensory integration difficulties, adapt your activities to meet the needs of these children or adapt their degree of active participation in the activity.

Basic Categories of Modification

26. For children having difficulty with age-appropriate activities, reinforce the skills needed for the activity by previewing the skills needed and preteaching these skills. If the children continue having difficulty, reteach the skills required to do the same type of activity at a future time.

27. If reinforcement does not help, try adapting the activity or the content of the activity to match the skills the child has developed.

28. If the demands of the activity or content are beyond the child's functional level at this point in time, plan a parallel activity for the child to engage in while the other children do the assigned activity.

29. Let the child participate to his degree of ability, but modify the expected outcome so the child can feel successful.

30. If a child can perform a task with adult or peer assistance, adjust the amount of assistance that the child receives, ranging from minimum to maximum assistance.

31. If it is important for a child to engage in the task other children are engaging in rather than creating a parallel activity, adjust both the task and the amount of assistance given to the child.

Brain Balancing

32. Children, as well as adults, can learn and perform better if they engage the use of their whole brain. This helps to balance of the functions associated with the left and right hemispheres of the brain. Using music for relaxation and doing certain types of movement activities can help facilitate this balance.

33. Drawing figure eights in the air helps balance both sides of the brain. To do this, have the children first draw figure eights horizontally in the air with their right hand three times. Second, repeat this using the left hand. As children are making figure eights, they are to follow their hand movements with their eyes. Then have the children use both hands going from left to right three times and then repeating from right to left three times. This activity can be done first thing in the morning and then repeated throughout the day as desired.

34. Refer to the book *Brain Gym*, listed in the Bibliography, for additional exercises to use for brain balancing.

35. Use visual, auditory, and kinesthetic input simultaneously to encourage and support the imagination of young children and to stimulate the use of the whole brain.

The previous list of strategies is just the beginning of the endless possibilities that educators in all settings and childcare providers can use to nurture the mental and social development of young children. The more attention paid to this aspect of children's growth and development, the more opportunities young children have to develop and use their abilities in the learning process. When a solid foundation for learning takes place in preschool and early childhood settings, children have a greater capacity for learning in their primary school grades.

The next four chapters will provide specific strategies to use in the areas of communication, small and large motor development, emotional and social development, and management and modification of children's behaviors.

[Please refer to Forms 4 and 5 in Appendix A for supplemental information.]

Chapter Four

Communication Strategies

Communication always occurs whenever two or more people share the same space. This communication can take the form of words, body language, facial expressions, touch, gestures, and/or pictures, whether we are aware of them or not.

When communicating with young children, it is important to pay attention to what messages we are sending to children through each of these forms of communication. Because young children are very perceptive in observing and sensing the messages we give through non-verbal types of communication, we need to be certain the words we use are consistent with our actions. If there is a discrepancy between the two, young children will respond first to the actions and secondly to the words used, or they may totally ignore the words when there is a discrepancy.

To communicate effectively with children, we also need to engage as many of their senses as possible as they tend to simultaneously use all of their senses. The degree to which we rely upon words as a communication form is dependent upon what we are communicating as well as the ability of the children to engage in verbal communication (understanding and responding). Strategies to communicate effectively with young children orally and also through the use of activities and materials will be addressed on the following pages.

Basic Communication Strategies

Communicating and interacting with others is dependent upon having the attention of the person(s) you are communicating with and engaging in the process of listening. For young children, one or both of these basic conditions may be difficult. Consequently, the adult needs to put effort into the process of bringing about successful communication.

Attending Strategies

36. Secure the attention of the child you wish to communicate with by verbally stating or showing your need for the child to look in your direction.

37. Secure eye contact with the child you wish to communicate with by using words and gestures to direct the child to look at your eyes.

38. Direct the child's attention to you or the object you wish the child to pay attention to by having another child or a small group of children demonstrate the appropriate attention behaviors.

39. Use sound (bell, drum, clapping of hands) while simultaneously pointing, to call the child's attention to the person or object you want him to attend to.

40. Engage a child's interest in what you will be saying or doing by first approaching and participating in what the child is doing and then moving on to the place where you need the child to participate next.

41. Engage a child's interest in what you are saying and/or doing by using both verbal and visual stimuli to call the child's attention to your request.

42. If the child does not respond to your verbal and/or visual approach, use touch to engage the child.

43. When working with a group of children, scan the group to determine whether you have secured the attention of each child.

44. For children who have difficulty "tuning in" initially, have the child sit next to a child who will be a good model for him.

45. Cue the child who is not focusing his attention to where it is needed, by calling attention to one or more children who are modeling the behaviors you desire.

46. Use positive affirmations to reinforce the engaging and attending behaviors of children who respond appropriately to your request with words such as, "I really like how Billy, Susie, and Mary are showing all of us a good way to get ready for the next activity we will be doing."

47. Reinforce appropriate engaging and attending behaviors through facial expressions (smiles are great for young children) and gestures.

48. To secure group attention at the completion of one activity and transition to the next, develop signals such as three hand claps, switching the light off briefly and then turning it back on, going to a certain place in the room, or playing appropriate music.

Listening Strategies

49. Model good listening habits for children by maintaining good eye contact (you may need to get down to the child's eye level), by hearing the child out without interrupting, and by giving feedback to show you understand the meaning of what the child is saying.

50. When working with children, note the balance or imbalance in the ratio between adult talking/listening as compared to child talking/listening. If this ratio is out of balance, make changes to bring about a better ratio. This process helps children feel valued and provides a model for talking and listening interactions.

51. Create a listening environment in the classroom by eliminating distractions as much as possible.

52. With children who get anxious about not being heard, assure them that each of them will have a turn at sharing.

53. Establish ground rules for listening. These may include allowing only one person to speak at a time while the others listen, looking at the person who is speaking, etc. Have children participate in the process of creating these ground rules as well as practicing them.

54. Provide a variety of listening experiences for children. These might include listening to music and listening to the sounds of nature.

55. Create a variety of listening experiences in which children close their eyes, listen carefully to what they hear and then try to make mental pictures of what they have heard. Provide a time or way (or both) for children to share what they have heard and seen mentally.

56. Speak to children in a natural voice using an appropriate volume. If a child does not hear you because he has been inappropriately noisy, do not raise the volume of your voice. Stop and wait until the child decreases his volume of noise and then proceed.

57. Adjust the pace of your speaking to allow most of the children to follow what you are saying. Encourage children to do this in their interactions with you and other children also.

58. State a purpose for listening when appropriate. This helps children listen for something rather than just looking like they are listening. This strategy helps children really "hear" what is being said.

59. In small group interactions, use the idea of a "talking stick," an object that is held by the child or adult who is speaking. Only the person holding the talking stick can speak. Others are expected to listen to that person until the talking stick is passed to another person. Start with very short periods of time and increase the time as children increase their ability to listen.

60. When communicating through the use of words, be certain the words are within the comprehension of the children with whom you are communicating. When words are out of a child's range of understanding, there is no incentive for the child to listen.

61. Encourage parents to be models for listening at home and to encourage their children to be good listeners during meal times and while engaging in family activities.

62. Provide a variety of activities to encourage active listening in young children during the time they are with you. Create specific listening goals for each of these activities. Children need regular practice and appropriate modeling to become good listeners.

63. Take the time to access some of the recent magazine articles and books on developing listening skills in young children for ongoing ideas to use to facilitate active listening among children in your setting.

Attaching Meaning to Print and Words

64. Young children respond best to strategies that are an outgrowth of the context of their everyday experiences. Play, the use of toys, and engaging in tasks that are child-initiated provide a wealth of opportunities for adults to promote the learning of communication skills. Utilize the experiences and objects common to children's lives for planning the strategies you can use to facilitate the development of children's communication skills in attaching meaning to print and words.

65. Children who have difficulty attaching meaning to print and words benefit from an approach called "prompting." Prompts are given by someone (usually an adult) before or as a child attempts a skill. As soon as the child learns the skill, withdraw the prompt.

66. Observe children interacting with other children, materials, and activities to determine the level of expressive communication at which each child is functioning. Use this as a reference point for developing and implementing strategies based on each child's needs.

67. Observe each child having difficulty in communicating to determine which body language, gestures, speech sounds, and/or words he uses to communicate what he needs or wants. Document these observations for all of the adults working with this child.

68. Plan appropriate communication goals for each child whose level of expressive language is below the expectation for the child's chronological age. Remember to develop goals that reflect the general order of expressive language development, starting from the simple to the complex, single responses to multiple responses, visual to verbal, etc.

69. Develop a picture dictionary of common needs and experiences for children of the age group (+/- 6 months) for whom you are providing services. Have this dictionary available for children to use in communicating their needs and wants to you by finding and pointing to appropriate pictures.

70. Develop a series of visually oriented task cards that represent the sequence of steps to follow in carrying out a task. Use these task cards with children who have difficulty following a series of directions.

71. Demonstrate to all the children in your group how facial expressions, gestures, and body language act as effective, non-verbal ways to communicate with others.

72. Provide children with experiences that encourage them to use and tune in to non-verbal forms of communication. Sign language is a well developed expressive form of non-verbal communication and one with which children are already familiar (pointing, beckoning, etc.). Sign language also helps motor development and brain hemisphere balancing, while mandating the necessity for clear communication.

73. Teach children to use pantomime as a form of communication by having them put actions to movement and then having them interpret what they saw in words.

74. Encourage both verbal and non-verbal forms of communication among children by pairing children who have difficulty expressing themselves with children who can serve as models, during play and activity times when appropriate.

75. Have children communicate their needs to another child. The child who receives the message can then tell you what the message is so you can respond to the child

who initiated the communication (in the manner of the familiar "telephone" game).

76. For a child with minimal expressive verbal language skills, start with a sequence of showing him an object, next showing him a picture of the object, and then naming or labeling the object. After this process, place the picture of the object in a personal dictionary for each child who needs this approach.

77. Each day, present the child with an additional object, picture, name, or label. Add this to the child's personal dictionary. Review the other pictures in the dictionary daily by saying the name of the object and having the child locate it by pointing.

78. Perform an action for the children in your group. Show a picture of the action you have performed. Give a word label to your action. Pair the children up to take turns repeating this process.

79. Choose an action to perform for the children. Have someone find a picture that goes with the action and then label it with the appropriate words. When children become proficient at this, they can do it as a game with each other with a minimum of guidance from an adult.

80. Give a child a picture representing an action. Have the child perform the action and then label it.

81. As children begin visually to associate the appropriate word with an action or object through practice, remove the picture. Use a series of words as prompts to have children point to the word named and then describe the object or action that goes with the word.

82. Use a series of pictures to tell a story. Replace one picture at a time with the appropriate word until the story appears entirely in words. For very young children or children having difficulty with language, start out with a meaningful sentence, and ultimately work into a short story.

83. Using clay or play dough (the kind you make), have the children make their favorite animal, food, toy, etc. Next, have them draw a picture of it and then label it using inventive or actual spelling of the word. For a child with limited word knowledge and/or writing skills, have another child or an adult write the word for him.

84. Have children bring magazines from home. Using the pictures in the magazines, have them create their own picture dictionaries around a theme such as favorite foods to eat, favorite toys to play with, things they like to do, various expressions

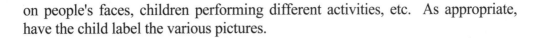

on people's faces, children performing different activities, etc. As appropriate, have the child label the various pictures.

85. Choose small groups of children to create a group picture dictionary using the same procedure as listed above. In this way, children with more highly developed communication skills can be models for the children whose skills are less well developed. This process also promotes opportunities for children to interact with each other to accomplish a group task.

86. The use of rhymes and songs provides an opportunity for children to become involved in language from a whole brain perspective, which is combining the functions of the left and right hemispheres. This helps facilitate language development. It also fosters the feeling of language as well as the thinking aspects of language. Incorporate these elements into the activities of the day with young children as often as you can, but no less than twice a day.

Strategies for Children with a Hearing Impairment

87. Consult with the professional who knows the child with a hearing impairment to learn the needs of the child. Determine the accommodations that need to be made for the child in the inclusive setting.

88. Always seat the child with a hearing difficulty near the speaker or at the center of any action involving verbal communication.

89. Use visual signals to secure the child's attention before initiating a conversation with the child, giving directions to the child, or asking the child to perform a certain task.

90. Face the child who has difficulty hearing, keeping your face within his view as much as possible, so he can read your lips and watch your facial expressions.

91. Speak and read clearly in a normal tone and at a moderate pace.

92. If a child is speaking too loudly or too softly, let him know, and then encourage him to speak within a normal range. You may have to demonstrate this for him through the use of gestures.

93. During small and large group discussions, repeat the questions and comments made, if necessary, for the child who has difficulty hearing.

94. If an interpreter is needed for a child, be aware of the positioning of that person relative to the demands of a task. For example, when a child needs to listen to the teacher, position the interpreter next to the teacher. When the child is working independently, the interpreter should be seated next to the child.

95. Pair verbal communication with visual aids, such as pictures, gestures, and demonstrations, etc. when communicating with children who have difficulty hearing.

96. Develop a series of picture cards for common directions you communicate verbally to children in your group. Pair these pictures with your verbal messages for the children who need this extra reinforcement.

97. Simplify your vocabulary, using as few words as possible to communicate a message or information to these children. An excessive use of words or the repetition of information verbally rather than by demonstration tends to overwhelm and confuse children with hearing difficulties.

98. Pair the child with a hearing impairment with a child who can model the behaviors needed for a specific task. Increase the success rate of the child with hearing difficulties by having him replicate the actions that are being modeled for task completion.

99. Make drawings or photographs of the steps for multiple-step activities. Keep these pictures on file for children to use as visual aids when needed to perform a specific activity.

100. When giving directions to a child with a hearing impairment, have the child repeat the directions back to you or to a peer to check for understanding.

101. For the child who has a hearing impairment, appoint a peer to cue the child when oral direction or information is given. Check for understanding as needed.

Strategies for Children with a Visual Impairment

102. Consult with the teacher or agency that is knowledgeable about the child who has a visual impairment to determine the child's needs relative to participating in an inclusion program.

103. Optical aids, such as enlargers or magnifiers, can be very helpful for children who are partially sighted. The use of these is dependent upon the child's degree of disability and the visual demands of the task. If there are any questions regarding the use of these, it is best to consult with someone who is trained in working with children who have a visual impairment.

104. If you use supplemental devices for one or more children in your setting, take the time to describe the devices (how they are used and why) to the other children in your group. This will help both the individual child and the other children to feel a part of the total group and also to learn about individual differences.

105. Lighting, both the angle and intensity, is very important for the child who has difficulty seeing. Evaluate the lighting under which the child does his tasks to determine the most effective situation for the child.

106. Allow the child extra time to complete his tasks, if needed. Be aware of visual fatigue during activities requiring continuous use of visual skills. Some signs of visual fatigue may include red eyes, rubbing of the eyes, laying the head down on the workspace, and squinting.

107. Minimize fatigue for the child by modifying the number and length of activities that require visual concentration.

108. When conversing with a child who has difficulty seeing, always address the child by name to help him cue into the interaction between the two of you. Also encourage the other children in your group to use this strategy.

109. Whenever possible, to decrease the risk of visual fatigue, parallel the visual activity with auditory input. Instruct the child to make mental pictures in his head while listening. Then have the child share these images with a peer or adult rather than writing his thoughts on paper.

110. Touch is very important for children who have a visual impairment. Provide these children with as many tactile experiences as possible to help connect with learning experiences.

111. For some children, colors placed over visual stimuli, such as pictures and print, help to enhance the contrast and darken the print so the visual demands on them decrease. Experiment with a yellow acetate overlay and with other colors to see which is the most effective.

112. When appropriate, use black flair pens to trace over print and pictures on the material used by children with dimmed vision. This helps to darken the print for them, making fewer demands on them visually.

113. Utilize the use of the child's sensory systems of touch, smell, and hearing as much as possible when communicating with children who have less highly

developed sight. This helps reduce the demands on the child's sight and also teaches the child to use other sensory systems in communicating with others.

Strategies and Information for Children with Limited Speech and Expressive Language

Many of the strategies listed above can be used effectively with children who have limited speech and expressive language. In addition, there are new assistive technologies available to use with this group of children. Such technologies, which exist in the form of devices and aids, enable children to be more independent in inclusive environments and to benefit from services provided by professionals. In many cases, both devices and strategies are needed for effective communication.

114. Currently, there are two basic types of aids or technologies in use:

> *Direct Selection Aids:* A technique or aid in which vocabulary takes the form of objects, pictures, symbols, or letters and words. To access this information, the child directly indicates his choice by using a finger, hand, eye gaze, pointer, or other means. Examples of this type include communication boards, communication vests, and E-trans devices. [See Appendix B for article entitled "Low-Cost Communication Devices for Children with Disabilities and their Family Members" for additional information on these devices].

> *Scanning Aids:* These consist of any technique or aid in which vocabulary items are offered to the child visually or auditorily and the child makes his choice by responding, usually with some type of switch. Examples of this type of device are the loop tapes (auditory-scanning voice output communication devices), communication clocks, compartmentalized communicators, and sequential scanners.

A new device on the market is the Neurophone. It was created by Dr. Patrick Flanagan for accessing sound via the skin rather than the ears. At this point, it appears to be effective for 50% of totally deaf people. [See the Bibliography to access more information about this device.]

Effective communication is critical in the lives and learning of children. New ways of accessing information and new ways of effectively interacting with one another will continue to challenge our creativity and ingeniousness. This chapter represents only the beginning of such an endeavor.

115. A variety of resources exists to assist childcare providers and teachers in their effort to achieve compliance with the Americans with Disabilities Act. To access these, call the American Speech-Language-Hearing Association (800-638-8255) to obtain information regarding auxiliary aids and services if there is no special education professional available. For information specific to a particular child, work with the local school district's speech/language pathologist who has expertise in augmentative and alternative communication.

[Refer to Form 6 in Appendix A for supplemental information related to creating a personal dictionary.]

Chapter Five

Large and Small Motor Development

Development of motor skills plays an important part in a child's social development and learning. Large motor development encompasses the movement of large muscle groups, such as arms, legs, etc., and precedes small (fine) motor development, which involves the use of hands and fingers. Since most motor activities have a visual component, a child's success in using his motor skills is also dependent upon his eye-hand coordination, referred to as *visual-motor integration.*

All children basically follow the same sequence of growth and development, but do so at different rates. Children with developmental delays and other identified disabilities often develop at a slower rate than their peers. The strategies in this chapter can be adjusted and modified to fit the needs of most children.

Strategies for Large Motor Development

116. Children will be at different levels in their mastery of the basic forms of locomotion, such as running, galloping, hopping, skipping, etc. If any children are significantly discrepant from their age expectation, make note of this and then chart their progress over the first few months of your program. If you see no improvement in skills relative to their initial reference point, consult with personnel from your local school district's special education department. In many school districts, this would be the adaptive physical education teacher.

117. Incorporate all the attributes of movement you can whenever you are planning large motor activities for children. These attributes include coordination, agility, balance, flexibility, strength, speed, and endurance.

118. Have children develop balance by providing a six-foot string or yarn stretched into a straight line on the floor. Let children practice their balance by taking turns walking on the line while placing one foot in front of the other.

119. As children gain their balance walking a six-foot line, have them increase their balancing skills by carrying various objects, first in one hand, then in the other, and then in both hands. Varying the size, weight, and shape of the objects will further improve their skills.

120. Using a six-foot string, create different shapes such as a circle, ellipse, figure eight, etc., to add interest and flexibility to the task of practicing balance by walking the pattern of the various shapes. Designing more complex shapes such as labyrinths (mazes) can be even more interesting and more challenging.

121. Children need practice throwing and catching objects. These exercises can and should be adapted so that each child experiences success in doing them. For example, in catching and throwing bean bags, some children may need to stand still and throw their bean bag gently into the air in order to catch them. Others can walk while tossing their bean bags into the air and catching them. Others can toss their bean bags back and forth to partners or among a group of children, while others with severe difficulties may have to stand with their hands forming a bowl and learn to grasp the bean bag that an adult or another child gently throws towards them.

122. By the time most children are four years of age, they are bursting with energy requiring motor activity as its outlet. It is important to allow them to fulfill their need for motor activity several times a day. Some of this can be during free activity time organized in conjunction with a playground or designated space within a building.

123. Add music to physical activities. Children can move to the rhythm of music spontaneously or in a planned sequence. Moving to music supports the development of motor abilities and often makes it more fun for the less physically involved children.

124. Simple dances are excellent for children in that they combine a number of skills such as listening, following directions, large muscle exercise, and body awareness.

125. Provide children with large blocks of many different shapes and sizes. With these they can be encouraged to build structures, roads, model cars, etc. which will help them see the relationship between objects and space. This is an important concept to teach children: that movement always has some relationship to space.

126. Give the children a variety of large toys that require the children to use their large muscle groups to manipulate.

127. Different movements of the arms and legs can be combined with walking. For example, have children practice moving the right arm simultaneously with the right leg and the left arm with the left leg while they walk. These movements can also be done in standing position or while lying on the floor.

128. Doing exercises that stretch the body not only gives the large muscles exercise, but helps the body develop greater coordination and more flexibility. Holding any one position momentarily can increase the body's endurance and strengthen the muscles used for each of the positions. Simple yoga stretches would be appropriate for most children.

129. Children who have delays in large motor development should be encouraged to participate in the activities at whatever level they are comfortable. Activities can be adapted to accommodate their lower skill level. Minimally, nearly all children can participate at the level of being an observer. Parallel activities using the same muscle groups, but at a less demanding level, may also be provided for these children.

130. Wheelchair participants should be encouraged to observe and participate at the level they can be successful. Some of these children may need to have adaptations made or special large motor activities designed for them by an adaptive physical education teacher or occupational therapist.

Strategies for Small Motor Development

131. There are an unlimited number of hand activities that can be used with young children to promote and support their small motor development. These can be made available through interest centers in the classroom where the children can work on them independently as well as through planned activities involving group participation. Having a variety of materials available for children to use during choice times also helps promote children's engagement in small motor activities. Some examples of activities for the development of eye-hand coordination include:

> *Stringing beads, macaroni, or circular cereal pieces.*
> *Using Legos and other small building materials.*
> *Practicing lacing shoes.*
> *Making vertical, horizontal, and diagonal folds with paper.*
> *Using pegboards, such as Light-brite, to create patterns.*
> *Screwing and unscrewing nuts and bolts.*

Practicing buttoning and unbuttoning.
Practicing manipulating snaps and zippers.
Using sewing cards to make a variety of designs.

132. Clay (or play dough) is a good medium for children to manipulate. For a beginning activity, children can roll the clay into long rolls to make clay pots or bowls by putting the long rolls in a circle and then stacking them on each other. Or, they can make individual letters and numbers from the clay rolls. Encourage the children to make other objects by rolling the clay into balls and creating other freeform figures.

133. Have children make telescopes by rolling up sheets of newspaper or colored construction paper, taping them in place, and then decorating them.

134. If a child has difficulty cutting with scissors, try a progression that begins with cutting a fringe on a piece of paper, cutting off the corners of a piece of paper, cutting simple shapes out of paper that have been outlined with heavy dark lines, or cutting out pictures in magazines which have been outlined with heavy black lines.

135. Have children tear different shapes or figures from newspapers or magazines and then create designs with these by pasting them on a piece of plain construction paper.

136. Have finger puppets available for children to use for creating dialogues or stories independently. Later encourage them to interact with other children to create group stories.

137. Sorting various shaped objects into similarly shaped containers helps children develop the small muscles of their hands. Have them do this sorting both visually and by touch (closing their eyes and feeling the shapes).

138. Have children practice paper weaving to make various designs. As they progress, they can create placemats for use in your setting or at their home.

139. The ability to use crayons and pencils will vary with chronological age and the small motor development level of the child. As a general practice, work from large crayons and pencils to smaller sized crayons and pencils.

140. If tracing around shapes and objects with a crayon is too difficult for a child, have him trace geometric shapes and other forms with his fingers. This will help both his sense of form and his visual-motor coordination.

141. Have children trace and then color shapes that gradually increase in complexity of outline. The degree of control of finger movements required of the children becomes greater as the outlines become smaller and more complex. This activity can easily be adapted to a parallel activity for children who have difficulty with fine motor tasks.

142. With dull scissors, have children cut pieces of clay or play dough into designs or familiar objects.

143. Cutting activities of all kinds help strengthen the hands and fingers of children in addition to providing eye-hand coordination practice. If a child has difficulty cutting, have him start out by cutting out large circles and then decreasing the size. Progress to more difficult shapes and then onto pictures as the child is ready.

144. Painting with water colors or tempera paints provides children with a fun way to develop and use their fine motor skills. Let them experiment with color, different shapes and forms, and pictures.

145. Use toothpicks to have children create different designs, objects, and figures (toothpicks make great stick people!). This is best done by having them glue toothpicks onto construction paper or lightweight cardboard.

146. Create sequences of finger movements. Demonstrate one sequence at a time and have the children repeat the sequence. Start out with a few finger movements in a sequence and gradually increase the number of movements per sequence as the children gain proficiency. Finger movements are good for finger dexterity, eye-hand coordination and sequencing. Making shadow forms on a back-lit wall adds the elements of mystery and interest to the exercise.

147. Mazes provide a fun way for children to develop their visual-motor abilities. Start with simple mazes, such as drawing a rabbit on the left side of a piece of paper, a carrot on the right side, and have the child draw a straight line connecting the two. You can create your own mazes to fit the range of visual-motor abilities within your group of children. See Form 7 in Appendix A for more examples of mazes.

148. Have children create mazes for other children to use. Run off copies of these mazes and have them available for the children to use during choice times.

149. Take the children out for a walk to collect one or two stones to bring back with them. Then have them paint an object, person, animal, or design on their stone.

150. Have the children collect small dry twigs from the ground of a nearby park. When you get back, encourage children to glue the twigs onto construction paper or lightweight cardboard to create designs and pictures. In a similar fashion, have them collect leaves and do the same project. As a variation, you can also have the children use both twigs and leaves for their pictures.

The above small motor activities help children develop eye-hand coordination skills that will later be applied to the writing process. An extension of these activities using crayons, pencil, and paper will be covered in Chapter 8.

Chapter Six

Emotional/Social Development

The emotional and social development of children plays a vital part in how they interact with the learning process. The development of emotional well-being and positive social relationships is the result of the combination of the innate qualities of children and their experiences with adults and children in their environments (refer to Figure 3 for a visual portrayal of this process). Emotional development is listed here before social development to reflect the concept that development starts from within and proceeds in an outward or external direction.

Play is as important to a young child as one's career is to an adult. It teaches the child what the world is like in miniature form and consists of valuable learning experiences. Play teaches children about themselves in relation to what they can and cannot do and to how they relate to people, objects, situations, and events. It is through play that the child practices the tasks of life. To accomplish this, the child needs the help and support of nurturing and caring parents, childcare providers and teachers. The strategies included in this chapter focus on children's emotional/social development, with play as the medium. The time commitment to the development of the emotional and social abilities of children should be in balance with the time commitment to their cognitive development.

Children with developmental delays and other special needs require a balanced focus on their emotional/social development to support them and give them the confidence to use their talents in ways that will enhance their learning without their getting discouraged or frustrated by their challenges.

Strategies for Supporting Emotional Development

151. For children to grow emotionally, they need environments that make them feel physically safe. This is accomplished by paying attention both to the physical facility relative to the safety of the children and to how they are treated by both adults and children in their environment.

152. Children feel emotionally safer in environments in which they know what to expect. Adults working in all settings need to have clearly thought out expectations that are communicated to the children in attendance in ways they can understand. This is particularly important for emotionally insecure children.

153. Consistency in expectations and structure for children in a childcare or school program helps children feel a sense of psychological/emotional security. This has to do with schedules for the day, changes in staff, and follow-through on commitments made to children. It is important for children to know in advance when changes are planned.

154. Pair up an emotionally insecure child with a child who is secure and feels confident about himself. This is especially important during less structured times, when introducing a new activity, and when leaving the building for an adventure.

155. Childcare providers and teachers should be aware of children's need to touch base with them frequently. It is best to pre-plan for this connection by providing children with appropriate ways and ample opportunities to do this. For shy children, adults will have to be the initiators of action rather than waiting for children to seek out a connection to touch base.

156. Giving genuine praise and positive affirmations to children while they are working on or completing a task gives less secure children the assurance that everything is okay. Praise often gives children the needed encouragement to persist in what they are doing and feel emotionally secure while doing it.

157. Feelings are very much a part of the inner world of children, who show these feelings by their behavior, facial expressions, and body language. Adults who work with young children can practice "reading feelings" by commenting to children about what they see and then observing their behaviorally and verbal responses.

158. Acknowledge children's feelings whenever they use feeling, related words and encourage them to describe what the feeling feels like inside of them. They may first connect with these feelings through the parts of their body such as having a stomach or head that hurts.

159. Teach appropriate feeling words to the children you are working with through the use of pictures, actions, and events that simulate the common experiences they encounter every day. Feeling words that young children can relate to include happy, sad, angry (mad), scared, excited, loved, and worried.

160. When children become more familiar with feeling words and can identify those mentioned above, expand their list to include feelings like fear, joy, peace, surprise, jealousy, caring, nervousness, and others as they come up during conversations and activities.

161. Use pictures to connect feeling words to their meanings when teaching these words to children. These can vary from simple facial expressions to complex actions that convey feelings through body language. Magazines are a rich source of pictures for children to explore for examples of different feelings.

162. Reading children stories where feelings are expressed helps them understand that all people have feelings, what the feelings are, and how those feelings are expressed.

163. Once children are able to attach labels to their feelings, it is important to work on how to handle them. If a feeling is positive children may simply need to share it with someone; if it is a negative feeling, help them to discharge the feeling in an acceptable way or to change it into something neutral or positive.

164. Have children name all of the animals they know. Make a list of these with one or more identifying feature for each. Have the children think about what each animal is like and then identify the one that reminds them (has some of the same qualities) of themselves. Children can then draw the animal and share with a small group of children why they chose the animal they did. This exercise helps children think about who they are and what qualities they have.

165. Encourage children to share their dreams with you and with each other. Dreams are one way in which children act out their feelings. To share dreams is a way children can get in touch with their feelings to understand better what is currently happening in their lives.

166. Carefully selected toys can be a medium through which children can engage their feelings and act them out. This can be done with an adult or other children. Puppets and other symbols of people, props that simulate experiences in children's lives, and stuffed animals are appropriate for this purpose.

167. Create quiet spaces and play spaces in your setting where children can choose to go to when they want to engage in solitary play or just be by themselves.

168. Begin the process of teaching empathy to young children by first having them relate to animals. For example, show them a picture of a bird and have the children imagine what it is like to be a bird. You can help children bridge the gap between themselves and take the perspective of others by repeating this process using any number of different animals.

169. Have a live animal in your setting whenever possible. Animals can provide bonding for all children, but more so for the child who is shy and unsure of himself in relating to other children and adults.

Strategies for Supporting Social Development

170. Promote social development in all children through the use of experiences, materials, and interactions with others. The situations will vary, depending upon the stage of social development of the child. This means providing for children who have not yet reached the age of symbolic play as well as for those who have moved into realistic and cooperative play.

171. Play is a natural, spontaneous activity for most children. Children with developmental delays in the area of social development will need to be encouraged by childcare providers and teachers to initiate interaction and participation with others. Pairing less socialized children with children who have good social skills is an effective way to start the socialization process for these children.

172. Symbolic play can initially be promoted by childcare providers and teachers by interacting with children in the following ways:

- When the child engages in play spontaneously, comment on what he is doing. Reinforce the child's play by making a positive comment about what he is doing.

- Imitate the child's action by engaging in parallel play with the child.

- Make indirect suggestions as to how the child may extend whatever he is doing by trying additional activities.

- Make direct suggestions to the child as to what he or the two of you can do with toys and other materials.

- Model symbolic play by initiating and showing the child what he can do with the play materials.

173. Toys are a viable, non-intrusive way of promoting social interaction between children with and without special needs. It is, therefore, imperative to have available a wide variety of toys that will interest children and will allow for children with physical limitations or other special needs.

174. Capitalize on children's natural interest in nature and animals to teach them some of the basic ideas about social behavior. This can be done by going out into nature and by observing how the various insects, birds, butterflies, etc., interact with one another. Watching a formation of Canadian geese or other birds or animals that flock together can be especially informative for children when followed up by questions and discussions. When doing this, encourage children to share their insights based on their creativity and imagination.

175. Use non-fiction and fiction stories about animals, insects, and birds for learning about the social habits of these creatures in nature and about how we can use some of those behaviors to develop social skills among ourselves.

176. Activities that require taking turns and sharing should be integrated throughout the child's day in all settings. For some children, these skills will need to be taught directly through modeling by other children and through talking them through the steps involved.

177. Dramatic play is an effective way to help children learn to feel and take the perspective of another child. By role-playing various parts, children experience what it is like to be someone else. The roles they play may be very different from who they actually are. Discussions should take place at the child's level of understanding to help them express what it was like to be someone other than themselves.

178. Take your dramatic play outside and use props provided by nature, adding them as needed to create various scenes, events, and stories.

179. Help children recognize and respond to the feelings of others by continually modeling these behaviors whenever you can. To assure that this takes place on a consistent basis, adults should have both planned times and spontaneous times when these behaviors are modeled.

180. Observe individual children to determine the types of interactions they use when playing or doing projects with other children. Watch for verbal/conversational interactions, motor/gestural interactions (such as waving, pointing, and turn-taking), or a combination of these. If a child is using one type at the exclusion of the others, or at a severely imbalanced level, make note of this. Plan how you can provide opportunities for this child to learn to use all of these interactions in more balanced ways.

181. Arrange social integration experiences requiring the least amount of adult direction and participation. This facilitates child-to-child interaction, as the shy child or less socialized child may tend to "shut down" when an adult comes onto the scene.

182. Teach problem-solving skills to children so that they can interact with each other independently of adults when it is appropriate. Problems that typically arise among young children include the taking of turns, sharing, cooperating for the good of the group, and resolving conflict in appropriate ways. Learning how to handle problems within the child's age expectation is important to their overall social development.

183. "What to do if..." kinds of situations help children learn that they have choices about how to respond in social situations, given certain conditions and behaviors by other children. Children can share their ideas in "what if" situations directly, or through role-playing various scenarios commonly found in social interactions. It is also important to practice the behaviors in simulated situations so that they can be more easily applied when actual situations are encountered.

184. Create a special place, such as a "peace table," where two children can go to settle their conflicts through the use of words rather than aggressive actions such as hitting. To do this successfully, children need to practice specific steps they can take to settle their conflicts whenever possible, these steps should be posted on the wall or table using pictures rather than words to convey the process for each step. Once children learn the process, they can be directed to go to the peace table when conflict arises. Eventually, most children will choose this way of settling conflicts independently.

185. Teach children assertiveness skills so that they will not be victims of other children's "bullying," either in a physical form or through the use of words. To do this, children may need adults to intervene when they see interactions heading toward trouble, stopping the behaviors and suggesting ways for children to compromise or to express their feelings in more appropriate ways.

186. After a conflict between children, ask those involved to replay what happened. Then help the children discover alternative ways of handling this situation by having them play out the situation in a more productive way.

187. Children form their opinions of their personal worth in a social context through their experiences and from the attitudes and behaviors directed toward them by others. To promote positive feelings of self worth, childcare providers and teachers need to create a variety of experiences and activities that allow different talents to emerge. Modeling a positive, constructive attitude toward all children encourages the children to do the same.

188. Give as much positive feedback to children as is warranted. When constructive criticism is needed by a child, give it privately, with a clear message that it is the behavior that is unacceptable, not the child.

189. Develop communication with the children to the extent that they are comfortable asking you or another child for help when it is appropriate. In giving help, use the attitude that you will show the child how to do something and support him while he is learning it.

190. "Self-talk" is internally directed, quiet verbalization of words. Teach children positive "self-talk" strategies that they can use while playing and working by themselves or with others to reinforce the message "I can do it."

191. Help children achieve positive self-esteem by modeling unconditional love and acceptance to them and by focusing on what is being learned or is done correctly rather than on what is not learned or is done incorrectly. As children observe and experience you doing this for them, they will begin doing it for other children.

192. Teach children to tune in to what makes them feel peaceful or calm and what makes them feel restless or jumpy. You can do this by playing different kinds of music and asking how they feel when each type is being played. Continue the discussion with the children by having them share which objects, activities, and people help them feel calm or peaceful. Encourage them to "mentally connect" (making pictures or hearing music silently) whenever they are feeling restless and jumpy as a way they can feel calm again.

193. Make a "peace center" somewhere in your setting where individual children can go when they feel upset, need to slow down, or just need to be by themselves for a brief time. In the space, have calming music available with headphones and soothing objects, such as stuffed animals, for the children to hold while they are there. Encourage children to choose someone in their setting to go with them to share the experience when it is appropriate.

194. As children are ready to understand intentions behind behavior, introduce this concept to them. Some actions can be labeled "helpful and appropriate" or "inappropriate" based on the intention of the act. For example, when a child touches another child, it can be with the intent of calling the child's attention to something positive, or it can be with the intent of annoying the child.

195. As children become more discerning, they will learn to react differently to the actions of other children when they are able to differentiate the intention behind the action. With young children, it is a good practice to start out by giving the individual the benefit of the doubt. This means that one makes the assumption that the intention behind the behavior was meant to be helpful, not hurtful.

196. When planning cooperative activities, games, and projects for young children, always build in opportunities for young children to become more socially aware and to develop their social skills. It is also important to respond spontaneously to "teachable moments" for increasing children's knowledge as social beings.

In conclusion, given sensitivity, knowledge, and experience, teachers and childcare providers can adapt most experiences and activities to meet the individual needs of children, regardless of where the children are in their emotional/social continuum of development.

Basic for all children, however, is the need to belong. According to Abraham Maslow, belonging is an essential and prerequisite human need that has to be met before one can achieve a sense of self-worth. Since a sense of belonging can only emerge in a social context, it is important that all childcare and school settings have a strong emotional/social component that builds on the strategies included in this chapter and other strategies found in the many other resources available to childcare providers and teachers.

[Please refer to Forms 8, 9, 10, 11, and 12 in Appendix A for supplemental information.]

Chapter Seven

Guiding and Modifying Children's Behavior

Behavior is a complex phenomenon which childcare providers and teachers work with every day as they interact with young children. Guiding and modifying this behavior is a large part of their job.

Placing emphasis on an approach emphasizing *guidance* rather than *discipline* for dealing with behavior helps children learn positive alternative ways of correcting inappropriate behavior. It also teaches them to solve problems in socially acceptable ways. The traditional discipline approach to managing behavioral problems may stop the inappropriate behavior, but it does not lead to learning socially acceptable ways of behavior or the developing of positive self-esteem.

General Strategies for Guiding Children's Behavior

197. Respond to the child's behavior as a form of communication. Ask yourself the question, "What information or feelings is the child trying to communicate to me?" Respond to the child to see if your understanding of what he is showing through his behavior actually results in the child changing his behavior. For example, if a child is feeling crowded and needs more space, he may act out or refuse to join in group activity. He may push himself into the group and cause problems for the other children. Acknowledging the child's need for space, you can prevent this problem by having him sit near the group without participating directly with it. Eventually, the child will learn to choose acceptable ways to handle his need for space independently, once he becomes familiar with his feelings and can identify them.

198. Think of a child's inappropriate behavior as mistaken behavior rather than misbehavior. The goal is to help the child learn from his mistake, not to punish him for making it.

199. Believe that negative behavior can be changed to positive behavior once the appropriate intervention or the best way to teach the child a new behavior is determined.

200. Separate the behavior from the child. It is the behavior that you cannot accept, not the child. According to Ginott (1975), adults need to address the behavior while protecting the personality of the child.

201. As a first approach to dealing with young children's mistaken behavior, assume they have not been taught the appropriate behavior. Teach them by modeling the necessary behavior and helping them to understand what to do in a given situation.

202. If a child repeatedly engages in mistaken behavior, look for possible reasons for the inappropriate reactions to everyday experiences and interactions with others. Possible reasons include:

- a mismatch of the child with his curriculum, his working materials, or his experiences
- difficulties in the child's life away from school
- the child has not been taught the appropriate behavior needed for the situation
- the child does not feel well physically due to inadequate nutrition or sleep, or because of health problems
- the existence of a neuro-developmental disorder

203. If stress or frustration is the primary reason for a child's poor behavior, consult with the child's parents to enlist their help in diffusing or eliminating the cause of the child's stress.

204. Observe the child behaving inappropriately to determine the degree of severity of the behavior and to see if there is any pattern present, such as certain times of the day, certain activities, etc. Make note of this. If a pattern emerges, evaluate what is usually happening during the times this behavior occurs and use that as your starting point for creating interventions.

205. Make a clear statement to the child that a problem exists and then encourage the child to use words to help solve the problem. For example, the adult might say, "We have a problem. Please use whatever words you can to tell me about what you think the problem is so we can solve it."

206. If a child does not understand the words chosen to help him solve the problem, demonstrate the appropriate behavior through gestures and facial expressions. Then demonstrate alternative appropriate behaviors for the situation.

207. Teach children acceptable alternative behaviors through the use of pictures. This can be done by creating pairs of pictures showing appropriate and inappropriate behaviors for given situations. When children are familiar with these and understand their meaning, use the pictures to cue the child to use appropriate behavior when you see him initiating an inappropriate behavior.

208. Use toy people and puppets to demonstrate acceptable behaviors for common experiences and events. Let the children replicate what you show them and expand upon your ideas. They may then role-play the same situations using children playing different parts to demonstrate appropriate behaviors in various situations.

209. Avoid the use of negative labels in talking with children about their mistaken behavior. Due to young children's limited development and experience, they tend to internalize negative comments, begin to see themselves as negative, and then respond accordingly.

210. Change poor behavior by first correcting it through teaching alternative behavior. If this is not sufficient to correct the child's behavior, use techniques that will be considered by the child to be helpful rather than punitive.

211. If the behavior that occurs is a group problem rather than an individual problem, use the classroom format to identify and explore alternative ways to solve the problem.

212. Videotape the behavior of an individual child or of a group during different times of the day. Help the child or children identify examples of appropriate behaviors. Do not identify any individual child's mistaken behavior publicly.

213. If a child is engaged in a mild, non-distracting form of inappropriate behavior, ignore the behavior. Point out acceptable behaviors by calling the group's attention to examples of appropriate behaviors in the given situation or circumstance.

214. Encourage children to work towards a change in their inappropriate behaviors by improvement in small steps if a total, immediate change is not achievable. Also, assure them that with continued practice, they will be able to reach the desired behavior in the future.

Strategies for Modifying Children's Behavior

215. For children who do not respond readily to teaching-type interventions to change their behaviors, a more extensive approach, often referred to as a behavior management plan, is needed. The goal of this plan is to weaken and eventually correct mistaken behaviors over a period of time.

216. Use the following steps to create a behavior management plan for a child:

Step 1. Make a list of the child's unacceptable behaviors for which you wish to create a behavior management plan.

Step 2. Prioritize the behaviors from high need for change to those least needing change. For young children it is best to work on one behavior at a time. Changing one behavior often results in the change of other behaviors.

Step 3. Decide on a goal for the specific behavior you want to change and the appropriate alternative behavior to replace it.

Step 4. Assess where the child is relative to where you would like him to be. Do this by establishing a baseline of the frequency of occurrence of this behavior by observing and recording how often the behavior takes place over a three-day period. You may wish to restrict the recording of behavior to a specific time period during the day.

Step 5. Decide on the intervention to use to help the child change his behavior.

Step 6. Every time the behavior occurs, immediately apply the intervention. Be consistent in using this intervention each time the behavior occurs.

Step 7. Record every time the targeted behavior occurs. Do this on the same chart you used to establish the child's baseline of frequency for this behavior. Your intervention is being successful if the behavior is decreasing in frequency. Keep in mind that habituated behavior often changes in small steps.

Step 8. Evaluate the effectiveness of the intervention. If there is little or no change in the frequency of the child's targeted mistaken behavior, try a different intervention.

217. When you are using a behavior management plan to change a child's inappropriate behavior to a positive behavior, use reinforcers such as social reinforcers (smile, touch, etc.), choice of activity options, rewards, etc., that are age appropriate and meaningful to the child whose behavior you are trying to change.

218. Use "time out" (where the child is sent to a designated place by himself) as a last resort. If you need to use this approach, all adults in the child's setting need to be consistent as to which behavior for a specific child warrants a "time out" period. The place used for a "time out" should be very dull to the child. Any "time out" for a young child should consist of no more than 1-5 minutes (the purpose of the "time out" for a young child is to stop a behavior or to re-direct the behavior to a more appropriate form).

219. For a child who needs "time out" as an intervention, teach him ahead of time that the purpose of the "time out" is to allow him to gain control of his behavior. Use "time out" as a supportive learning tool rather than as a punishment.

220. When a "time out" is needed for a child, follow these steps:

1. Briefly tell the child why he is getting "time out," i.e., he hit Joey.
2. Do not lecture or demean the child.
3. Calmly escort the child to the designated "time out" location.
4. When the child's time is up, simply direct the child to rejoin the other children.

221. If you need to take action to stop a behavior, use signal interference. Let the child know he is doing something unacceptable by a raised eyebrow, a frown, or a shake of your head. Define limits succinctly and reasonably, with consequences clearly understood. If improper behavior occurs, activate the consequences immediately following the behavior. Be consistent in doing this whenever the behavior occurs.

222. If you have tried several approaches with little or no success in changing a child's erroneous behavior to socially acceptable behavior, inform the child's parents and cooperatively seek out other resources to help the child.

Strategies for Children with Attention Problems

223. Attention problems exist in several forms: not being able to focus attention on a purpose or task, inability to sustain attention for a period of time, and impulsiveness or distractibility. However, it is important to keep in mind that many young children display some of these behaviors as a function of their age and their response to informal and formal structure in the preschool setting. For

these children, it is important to teach them ways to adapt to the environmental demands.

224. For the children who demonstrate an excess of these behaviors, more extensive interventions are needed to help them increase their focusing and attending behaviors. The use of medication as an intervention is generally not advised for young children. Therefore, it is up to the adults in a child's life to work with these behaviors through appropriate interventions.

225. Certain colors have been found to have a positive effect in helping children feel calmer and to help keep their attention longer. To use this intervention, have several colors available in your setting. Different colored construction paper and carpet squares are easy to obtain and use. Have an assortment of these available so that children can select the color that makes them feel calmer and more comfortable. They can use their color to sit on, place beside them while they are working on a project, use as a placemat, etc. Since young children are very changeable, they need to be able to select the color that makes them feel good on a daily basis or more often if needed.

226. Always obtain a child's initial attention through eye contact.

227. For children who are easily distracted, plan for their seating and work area to be away from the potential distractions caused by being close to a window, near a main traffic pattern of the room and other distracting children.

228. Reduce the amount of external stimuli in your setting whenever appropriate. Hanging mobiles and having an excessive number of pictures and objects around activity areas add to the distraction factor for children who have difficulty paying attention and staying on task.

229. Children who have attention difficulties need consistent routines and more structure than other children. The degree to which they need these is dependent upon their inattentiveness relative to their age expectation.

230. Play music that is relaxing during transition times to help calm children and move them into a new task or project more comfortably. Music can make children less vulnerable to distractions.

231. Children who have attention and distraction problems do better when working in smaller groups rather than larger groups. Whenever possible, use a small group approach for activities with these children. Ideally, start with groups of three and gradually increase the group size as children are better able to focus and sustain attention.

232. Give one-step or two-step directions. Check for understanding of each step. When possible, pair visual demonstrations with verbal input.

233. Give the active child only one thing to do at a time.

234. Use a timer to assist the child in remaining focused. Set the timer to coincide with the amount of time you perceive the child is able to sustain attention. Start with short periods of time and gradually increase the time as the child increases his ability to concentrate.

235. Allow the active child many opportunities for physical movement throughout the day. Individual and group play times help achieve this goal for the child.

236. If you sense the activity level of the group of children is increasing, stop whatever the children are doing. Have the children relax in place for one minute. A rag doll posture or other relaxing postures along with deep breathing (from the stomach) have a calming effect on children. These procedures may need to be used more often for the higher energy children in your setting. The eventual goal is for children to sense when they need to stop and relax, initiating this activity for themselves.

237. Young children naturally talk to themselves while engaging in play and other activities. Encourage children to use this self-talk technique to help themselves stay calmer and more attentive to what they are doing.

238. Pair active children with calm children for parts of the day that require the most concentration. Do this also when assigning children to groups. Balance the types of children you place in each group.

239. Allow the active child to have only the necessary materials for his current activity or project at his work space. Also, allow the child to either stand or sit while working. Often an active child prefers to stand and be able to be more mobile.

240. Have a variety of stuffed animals available for children to hold during listening times. Cue them to listening by telling them their responsibility is to teach the animal to listen by how they listen.

241. Children should receive frequent accolades for their efforts to listen, pay attention, and stay with an activity for appropriate periods of time. This can be done through the use of words, gestures, and facial expressions. If a child does not respond to these social rewards, you may need to consider a "token" system. Here a child can earn tokens for special privileges in your setting or in the home setting. Rewarding the child when he is engaged in appropriate behaviors gives him the message that he can be successful. It also reinforces repetition of the

behaviors you expect from the child. Although this may be helpful initially, extensive use of material rewards is not recommended.

242. When the child with attentive, impulsive, or distractive behaviors is engaging in inappropriate behavior, tell him what he should be doing instead of what he should not be doing. This helps the child understand what is expected of him and avoids setting the child up to engage in another inappropriate behavior.

243. A child who has attention problems should be given ample opportunity for success to teach him he can control his behavior.

244. Keep a positive attitude toward children with attention difficulties. Acceptance, encouragement, and acknowledgement of their strengths are important for them to have a positive attitude about themselves. This serves as a foundation for all social relationships and all learning behaviors.

Strategies for Aggressive and Withdrawn Behaviors

Aggressive Behaviors

245. Hitting, non-compliance (where a child does not comply with an adult's request), and teasing are behaviors exhibited at times by most young children. The child who is considered aggressive demonstrates one or more of these behaviors more frequently and/or in situations where these behaviors are not acceptable. In working with this type of child, identify the aggressive behaviors, the frequency and severity of the behaviors, and in what context the behaviors take place.

246. View aggressive behavior as learned behavior. As such, it can be modified and changed through a learning process, given the correct interventions. The adult's responsibility is to find what works for a particular child.

247. Develop a word list of what you consider to be aggressive behaviors. Find pictures that illustrate each of the behaviors you have identified and match these with the word list. Share this list with the children and talk about why these behaviors are not acceptable in your setting. Post this list in an appropriate place as a reminder for the children who need it.

248. When a child persists in engaging in aggressive behaviors, consult with the child's parents to determine whether these behaviors also occur in the home and neighborhood settings. If so, work cooperatively with the parents to find effective and consistent ways to intervene with the intent of decreasing aggressive behaviors in all settings. If the child does not display these

behaviors in any other setting, evaluate what is happening in your setting to put these behaviors into motion.

249. Use a behavior management plan, such as the one mentioned previously, to decrease and eventually eliminate aggressive behaviors. "Time out" is also an effective intervention for children with aggressive behaviors. In all cases, be clear about the consequences of the behaviors and be consistent in using them.

250. Intervene early. If you see a potentially explosive situation, get to the child quickly to help him regain control. Use your presence, where you physically go to the child and either stand or sit by him rather than talk to him from across the room.

251. When you stop to re-direct a child's aggressive behavior, do so calmly and in a matter-of-fact way. Help the child regain control by your calm, controlled manner.

252. In group discussion, talk about ways children can express their feelings in non-violent, non-aggressive ways, such as using words instead of actions, or talk to the children about what is happening to them and ask them how they feel about it.

253. Give children true-to-life, concrete examples when discussing these issues. For example, you might suggest, "Suppose Ann poked you. What would you do? What are all the things you could do that are non-violent to let Ann or an adult know how you felt about being poked?"

Withdrawn Behaviors

The withdrawn child generally spends as little time as possible with other children or adults, especially when he is in settings away from his home. When in the presence of others, this child either engages in independent, parallel play or simply observes the others without participating.

Group situations compound the difficulty for the withdrawn child. When someone talks to him, he is unlikely to respond, or if he does, he will limit his answer to one or two words. It is difficult for this child to make eye contact or smile at another adult or child other than his family. This behavior becomes even more extreme in the presence of others. For this type of child, toys, books, and other inanimate objects are more comforting and less threatening than people.

254. If you have a withdrawn child in your setting, it is important to talk with the child's parents to determine how their child relates to others in the home and neighborhood settings. If possible, find the cause for the withdrawn behaviors. Check if the child has been shy or withdrawn from birth or if this is a more

recent occurrence, i.e., at the onset of attending preschool, after some trauma, etc. The reason for these behaviors could also be due to lack of exposure to social situations, the pressure of cultural expectations, the personality of the child, or how the child was treated when he initially tried to communicate or interact.

255. Sometimes withdrawal is a way for a child to avoid a painful situation based on the child's previous experience with people. Determining the cause can help the adults working with the child to create ways of encouraging him to begin to participate in social and task situations.

256. Encourage the shy or withdrawn child to participate initially at the level of communication that is most comfortable for him. This may involve the sharing of pictures with no verbal interaction. If the child attempts communication at this time, pay close attention to him and encourage his participation.

257. Accept where the child is and proceed from that point in helping him interact to a greater degree with his environment.

Strategies for Problem Solving

258. Teaching problem solving to young children at a level that is appropriate for their experience and age encourages them to respond to their world with a sense of competence and independence. Included in the problem-solving process is the ability to make decisions. This, too, can be taught to young children. The first step in implementing this process is to be aware of the daily life experiences of children and the challenges that these experiences generate. This should be the context in which problem solving and decision making are taught.

259. Read stories to children about the kinds of situations similar age children encounter in their every day life. Introduce various types of situations to the children and discuss with them how most children respond to these situations and successfully work them out. Children can then share some of their own experiences and explain how they were resolved.

260. Create a series of situations, either verbally or through pictures, where children are engaged in experiences that require problem solving. Have children role-play the various situations, generating as many solutions to a problem as they can. Have each child share which solution feels best to them, helping them put their feelings into words.

261. Use games to provide children with practice in decision making and problem solving.

262. For the child who has difficulty making decisions, narrow his choice to two options, and then have him choose the one he prefers. Gradually increase the child's options until he becomes comfortable with making decisions. Eventually his decision-making skills will improve, as will his confidence in himself.

263. Teach a simple problem-solving process to the children. The basic steps to this process include:

   1. recognizing that a problem exists
   2. using pictures (facial expressions) to show how having the problem makes him feel
   3. using words to share the problem with someone else
   4. thinking of ways to solve the problem
   5. choosing one thing to take action on and
   6. trying it out to see if the problem gets solved

264. Provide a variety of opportunities and experiences for children to practice decision-making and problem-solving skills. Let the children who grasp the idea quickly help the children who have more difficulty with this process.

265. Support children in their efforts to make their own decisions and solve the problems they encounter, even when the result is not successful.

266. Encourage parents to promote decision making and problem solving in the home setting, reminding them to provide the necessary guidance for their child to be successful.

Children's behaviors are purposeful and meaningful to them and are an important way in which they communicate with others. Adults need to tune in to the behaviors of children, interpret what they mean, and then respond accordingly. When children's behaviors take the form of mistaken behaviors, it is the adult's responsibility to note the current behavioral level of the child and intervene to transform inappropriate behavior into socially acceptable behavior. The strategies listed in this chapter can form the basis for this process.

[Please refer to Forms 13, 14, and 15 in Appendix A for supplemental information.]

Chapter Eight

Preparatory Writing, Reading, and Math Skills

These skills are the foundation of future academic learning for all children. How these teachings are first presented to children influences the attitude they will develop toward learning. If educators or parents attempt to teach these skills in advance of a child's developmental readiness or in inappropriate ways, there is a likelihood that the child will be frustrated. This could result in a negative attitude toward future learning. Children with developmental and other disabilities are particularly vulnerable in this regard.

Current research about how writing and reading are learned, how children make sense of their world through playful exploration, and how the brain works all support the concept that writing and reading are outgrowths of the same need to communicate that children use to express themselves orally and pictorially. *Emergent literacy* is the term used currently to describe this process. As such, it is viewed as a natural developmental process that occurs in a sequence of stages for all children.

Environments rich in a variety of books, and adults who model a love for writing and reading best promote a child's natural urge to engage in these activities.

The preparatory math strategies included in this chapter are related to the concept of quantity, size, time, and measurement.

The emphasis of the strategies in all of these areas is on creating experiences in which children can explore and experiment with preparatory writing, reading, and math skills in ways that are consistent with a developmental point of view. Since the natural development of writing and reading occurs simultaneously in children, these two areas will appear together.

Preparatory Writing and Reading Strategies

267. A generally accepted sequence for the development of a child's writing proceeds from:

    1. pretending to write by scribbling horizontally, to
    2. scribbling in which the features of real letters appear, to
    3. the writing of real letters, to
    4. writing words with invented spelling, to
    5. writing words with actual spelling

Observe the level at which each child in your setting is performing, record the date of your observation, and watch for movement to the next level.
[Note: Children with developmental delays may not have started on the first level at the time of your initial observation.]

268. Set up a writing area for children with all the necessary implements, such as markers, crayons, pencils of varying sizes, unlined paper, lined paper with large spaces between the lines, tablets and pads of various sizes and colors, and colored chalk with small blackboards. Encourage children to experiment with the various materials you have provided when they have unstructured time. Let the participation be at the child's level of readiness.

269. Combine color and/or music with eye-hand activity whenever you can to expand the sensory stimulation of the experience. This increases the quality of the experience for the children and facilitates the integration of their motor activity.

270. Have a variety of colored paper and writing tools for children when they engage in scribbling or preparatory writing activities. Let them choose the combination of colors that feels the best to them.

271. Designate a place where children can go to listen to music with headsets while they are doing their scribbling and preparatory writing activities. Music that simulates the rhythm of the heartbeat is excellent for this purpose. It sets a steady, comfortable pace which is already an intrinsic part of the child.

272. Drawing circles, semi-circles, and straight lines in horizontal and vertical positions precedes combining these shapes into letters. Allow the children many opportunities to have fun making these forms using different colors and different media such as clay, sand trays (sand placed in trays), etc., in addition to drawing them on paper.

[Note: This activity can also be used as a parallel activity for children to use when other children have moved on to making actual letters.]

273. Provide the opportunity for children to "feel" the letters by having them put the letters into movement. To do this, they can lie on the floor and curl around to make the shape of each letter. Have them start out by making the easiest letters, such as O, L, C, etc. For children who cannot create the shapes of the letters on the floor, use masking tape and form letters for them on a table. Have them trace out the shape of each letter with their hand, naming it as they do so.

274. Pair children of about the same height together and have them form letters through the movement of their bodies. Music enhances these movements and makes this activity more fun. When children become proficient at doing this, have one pair of children do a movement for the rest of the children. Have the second group then guess what letter has been formed.

275. Have children practice writing in the air with their dominant hand, first with their eyes open so they can visually see the letter, and then by closing their eyes and feeling its shape.

276. Pair children and have them practice imaginary writing on each other's backs. Have them take turns doing this. Make a game out of this activity by having the child whose back is being written on guess what letter it is.

277. Use toothpicks to give children the opportunity to experience the shape of letters. Have them experiment with all the letters such as A and H that can be constructed with straight sticks. Later add circles and semi-circles so that they can experiment with making the letters requiring those shapes, such as O and C. Then progress with combining circles, semi-circles, and toothpicks for completing the most complex letters, such as B, D, etc.

278. Use a flashlight to write shapes and letters on the ceiling, chalkboard, or wall. Have the children track the light with their eyes and the pointing finger of their writing hand while they name the shape or letter.

279. Provide tactile writing experiences for children through group experiences and as an independent choice during unstructured time. Cut letters out of various grades of sandpaper which children can finger-trace with the pointing finger of their dominant hand. Use colored glue, glitter, pipe cleaners, seeds, etc. to create textured models for the children to finger-trace. Encourage the children to do finger-tracing with their eyes open until they are familiar with the shape of the letter and then with their eyes closed, visually seeing the shape of the letter in their head while finger-tracing the letter. It is also a good practice to

have them name the letter as part of the preparatory reading process while doing the finger-tracing and visualizing of the shape of the letter.

280. Have children experiment with using a different color for each letter when writing words singly or in sentences using inventive spelling.

281. To aid in their understanding of "left" and "right," first create a vertical list of words. Have them make the first letter of each word green, and the last letter red. Remind the children to start a word at green and stop at red.

282. Small trays filled with sand or rice provide a good alternative for a writing medium for children who have not yet developed the fine motor control necessary to manipulate a pencil.

283. Encourage children to make shapes and letters with watercolor paints and brushes, working either from an easel or while sitting at a table. Using watercolors also gives them an opportunity to experiment with color.

284. Give children the opportunity to practice their fine motor skills by providing tracing paper and objects, shapes, and letters for them to trace.

285. Use games to encourage children to experiment with the letters of the alphabet, by playing with magnetic letters, letter dice, and other forms of letters.

286. Create or purchase alphabet cards having a picture of an object on them. Let the children make up games such as finding the first letter of their name, matching letters, etc. This can be done independently by one child or done in small groups.

287. Provide the children with a choice of alphabet books that have interesting and meaningful objects to go with each letter or word. When children are ready, encourage them to make their own alphabet books.

288. Have available computer alphabet programs that are specially designed for young children to learn letter recognition in a simple, fun way, not as lessons. Programs that have animated graphics and music are especially appealing to young children.

289. Label different areas and objects in your setting with colorful signs. This helps connect the child with the idea that words have meaning. Encourage children to make their own signs for their work areas or for their room at home by setting aside a special table with materials and letter templates.

290. Have each child decorate a shoe box that can be used as his individual mailbox at school. Have him print his own name on the box. If the child cannot do this, have an adult either do it or provide him with a stencil for printing his name. To help children understand that print has meaning, leave brief notes in each child's mailbox on a weekly or bi-weekly basis. These can be translated by an older sibling or a parent at home, or by an adult in the school setting.

291. Create a series of cards that have pictures of an action on them, such as stand, sit, smile, frown, etc. Label each card with the action word that best describes it. Take a few minutes each day to have the children perform some of the actions by holding up one card at a time. As they perform the action, have them say the word or words that go with the action. This exercise helps children link words with actions.

292. Based on her research with preschool children, Judith A. Schickedanz proposed the following sequential stages of children's natural development in the area of reading:

    1. retells stories from books with increasing accuracy
    2. shows awareness that print in books tell a story
    3. attempts to match telling of story with print in book and
    4. wants to know what particular print says.

To determine where each child is in his knowledge of natural reading skills, observe the child's interaction with books and stories. This can be done when children engage in imaginary play that is based on the information found in a book, or when two or more children share a book.

293. Bring children and books together by having a large variety of books available for children to look at and share with each other. This collection of books should be composed of make-believe stories, stories about animals, nature stories, and stories about young children and their daily adventures and challenges, and should be filled with colorful pictures.

294. Encourage children to bring their favorite books from home to share with the other children. Set aside a specific time each week when children can do this.

295. Remember, children love the familiarity of repetition and benefit from listening to their favorite stories over and over. Soon they take on telling the story in their own words, practicing the natural sequence of preparatory reading skills that match the telling of a story with the actual print in the book.

296. Invite people from the community to come and read to the children in your setting. Prepare guidelines for the visitors to use when they read to your group of children.   Unless the visitor has had experience working with young children, it is best to provide the person with a book to read.

297. For the children who are ready for more extensive experiences in writing, provide them with the materials and support to engage in mock letter writing, using inventive spelling to write one-to three line-stories.   Then have them read their story to another child, to a small group, or to one of the adults in your setting.

298. Before you read a new story to children, draw them into the context and experience of the story by focusing on one or two pictures in the story through a series of questions.   Lead-in questions can be:

- Who and what do you see in this picture?
- What is happening in the picture?
- What do you think will happen next?
- What colors do you see in the picture?
- How do you feel when you look at this picture?
- What parts of the picture remind you of other stories you have heard or something that has happened to you?

299. Provide a tape recorder and some blank audio tapes in a special place in your room for children to use when making up their own stories.   Teach the children to operate the tape recorder so that they can use it when they have a story to tell.   Have them tell their story into the tape recorder, then give you the tape to transcribe their story for them.   Give them the printed copy of their story and have them read it to you.   They may want to illustrate their story and put it in a booklet form, to be added to as they create additional stories.   If children really get into this activity, you may ask a parent to volunteer once or twice a week to do this project with the children.

300. After a field trip or other event, have the children share their experience by writing a story about it.   Do this as a group and combine as many of the children's ideas as you can into the story. Once the story has been printed in words by you or another adult, post the story on the wall so that the children can practice reading the story on their own.   They will read it by memory and put their own thoughts into the story. This will help them connect with the meaning and purpose of print and reading.   If you have other adults available in your setting, creating small groups of children to write their experiences in story form is more effective than doing this activity in a large group with young children.

301. Read rhymes to children often. Choose a variety with differing rhythms. Once the children become familiar with the rhythms, have them clap to the rhythms while you read.   To extend this experience, provide the children with simple percussion-type instruments such as sticks, bells, dried gourds, or small drums to use while you are reading the various rhymes.

302. When children become familiar with rhymes and can repeat some from memory, have them make up their own rhymes. Working as pairs often facilitates this process for children. Invite children to share their rhymes with other children and with the whole group.

303. Encourage the children to combine singing and/or musical instruments with the words of their rhymes when they share them.

304. Combining singing games with simple folk dances translates words and music into actions for children. These help children expand their vocabularies and help make words a fun part of their lives.

305. Word games are appropriate to use with young children when they can match and identify simple words. Word blocks and word bingo are examples of the types of games that can be used. Word blocks consist of a series of small plastic or wooden blocks with simple words pasted on their sides. Children use the word blocks to make up simple sentences. In word bingo, typical bingo cards are used, but simple words are pasted over the numbers. The number cards also have matching words pasted on them so that when a word is drawn, the child looks for the word on his bingo card. The same rules are followed as for regular bingo with numbers. A completed bingo card should consist of simple sentences.

306. Provide a variety of props for children to use in dramatic play. Encourage them to make up their own plays and perform them for the other children.

307. Read a variety of poetry to children. Invite a local writer of children's poems to come to your setting and read his poetry to the children. Have the poet share what it feels like to write and to share his poetry with others. As a follow-up, have a poetry-writing session with the children where they write short poems. To help young children choose what they want to write about, have them think of their favorite animal, toy, or object, and then have them write a few sentences about it in a poetry format. For children who cannot write real letters, let them use scribbling or mock writing and then tell an adult what they wrote so the poem can be transcribed into words.

308. Young children love to learn and use new words. Take as many opportunities as possible throughout the school day to call attention to a new word that comes up from experience. Also, plan to introduce the children to at least one new word each day, giving them the word in picture form, in action form when possible, and in word form. When appropriate, connect feelings with the word.

Give as many examples as possible of how the word can be used in their daily lives.

Preparatory Math Skills

309. Numbers should be introduced to children in the context in which they occur, such as in a child's age, on signs children see while traveling to and from school, on clocks, on calendars, in stores, etc. Have the children tell you where they see numbers being used in their everyday experiences. Make a list of these and have the children add to them as they discover additional places. Discuss the different ways in which numbers are used and what kinds of information we get from them.

310. Increase children's awareness of numbers and their one-to-one correspondence with quantity by telling them the names of numbers. Start out with 0 and add additional numbers as the children are ready. Carefully and clearly define the quantity associated with each number. This is best done by introducing objects, showing them pictures of the objects, naming the number of objects, and then writing the numerical symbol that represents the number of objects.

311. Use coarse sandpaper to make the numbers 1 to 9. Have children take turns feeling the shape of each number. Let them share what the shape feels like and use words to describe the shape. For children who have difficulty writing, have them place a piece of paper over the letter and rub a crayon over the letter shape to make an impression of the letter on their paper. Then have them cut out the number and keep it for future use.

312. Have each child choose his favorite number and draw or write it on his favorite color of paper. Often a child will choose the number of his age, so have several copies of each number for the children to use as models.

313. Play a matching number game by having each child use his favorite number to find the other children in the room who have the same number. When they have found all the children who have matching numbers, have those with the same numbers sort the numbers by color.

314. Collect shells, beads, seeds, various shaped pasta, and buttons. Put them into boxes or bags. Use these collections to sort and classify objects.

315. Use egg cartons or muffin tins to give children the opportunity to experiment with sorting objects. If you paint a number on each section, these can also be used for children to practice counting out the number of objects as it corresponds to the number written on each section.

316. Plan activities to help children become familiar with the terms same, different, more, less, small, big, or large. These terms are the abstract distinctions of numerical values.

317. Create opportunities for children to use counting in as many ways as possible throughout the day. During snack time, they can count the number of napkins and cups needed for each table. They can count the number of children at each table or in each work space. They can count the number of different toys they use during free play time, etc.

318. Have children practice making numbers by having them use the same techniques they used to make letters, only substitute numbers for the letters. Be sure there are plenty of examples of correctly made numbers available for the children to look at as models for their numbers.

319. Choose appropriate computer games for the children that will help them gain a better understanding of counting and the one-to-one correspondence between numbers and quantity. A game approach is better for young children than a skill approach.

320. An abacus serves as a wonderful introduction to numbers, as it is physical in form, yet abstract in concept. It was used as the first calculator and still provides a functional means for working with numbers.

321. Sequence and order are important for children's understanding of math processes. To let children experience these two concepts, provide them with "connect the dot" games for creating objects and pictures.

322. Set up a treasure hunt within your room or on the playground. Use a sequence of numbers as clues for locating the treasure. Restrict the range of numbers to the ones that are familiar to most children. Children also enjoy setting up treasure hunts for each other.

323. Make a pictorial representation of the schedule the children will be following each day on a large calendar (weekly or monthly). Divide it into a.m. and p.m. Check off each activity on the schedule as it is completed. This helps children feel a sense of sequence and order as they progress through the day. Numbering each activity gives children further experience with the sequence and order of numbers.

324. Construct games using popsicle sticks, beads, buttons, etc. to help children experiment with making associations between a number and its quantity. Allow children to experiment creatively with these in the ways they use them and in making up games from them.

325. Use singing games and rhymes, such as "one, two, buckle my shoe," or "one little, two little, three little kittens," to help children experience numbers and their sequence in a variety of contexts.

326. Children can experience time (and distance) by finding the answers to questions through physical action. For example, will it take longer to walk or to run to that tree? To demonstrate the difference, have two children line up an equal distance from the tree. Have one child walk while the other child runs to the tree. As children observe the outcome, they will be able to answer the question. Repeat this same procedure using different end points, different directions, and different objects to let children experience time and distance from this perspective.

327. Give children measuring (spatial) experience by having a sand tray (or one filled with rice), measuring cups, and measuring spoons available for them to experiment with the various sizes and the quantities they hold. Create a series of pictorial cards comparing the different sizes. Have the children determine which holds the most sand/rice, which holds the largest, and which holds the smallest amount, which is the biggest cup, the smallest spoon, etc.

Preparatory writing, preparatory reading, and preparatory math activities for young children should be based on their level of applicability. There are unlimited fun-filled activities from which to choose. The strategies and activities listed here are just a sampling.

Chapter Nine

Assessing Young Children

Assessment is a process whereby we systematically gather information about children from a variety of sources. When assessing young children, we need to be cognizant of their developmental patterns so that the types of assessments we use give us the most accurate results. The standards set by the school system should not solely determine what testing young children undergo. Certain situations may require the gathering of information about a child that goes beyond what schools require. Assessments for children should include both standardized and informal measures of their functioning in a variety of areas to gain an understanding of the "whole child."

Accurate assessment requires not only expertise, but also sensitivity on the part of the adults who participate in this process. Hunches and a sense of knowingness (often referred to as intuition) also play an important part in the assessment process. The following pages will detail some of the issues that arise in the assessment of young children and will offer strategies that can be used to accomplish this task.

Characteristics of Young Children That Affect Assessment

Young children can be unpredictable in their reactions and behaviors to people and situations in their environment. Their responses can shift on a moment-to-moment basis. This affects the accuracy and reliability of assessment data and raises the question as to whether a small sample of the child's behavior represents a true picture of the whole child.

328. Young children are often unable to explain themselves well. They demonstrate what they know and how they feel through their behaviors, rather than through words. Adults, therefore, must infer a child's thoughts and feelings from the child's behaviors.

329. A short attention span is typical of young children. This means that adults need to be patient, work with the child in short segments of time, and gather their information over an extended number of days.

330. Language is understood and expressed by young children at a very literal and concrete level. In assessing children, the adult should use a minimum of words that are at the level of the child's understanding.

331. Young children respond more readily to people, objects, and situations within a natural context. Assessment should take place in and utilize the resources of the child's normal environment whenever possible to ensure the authenticity of the results of the assessment.

Developmental Patterns

Growth begins and proceeds from the inner world of the child and is then expressed in the external world. In assessing young children, we can only measure the external manifestations of their inner growth processes. Sometimes we can get a hint of an emerging skill if we pay close attention to the qualitative aspects of a child's responses. When assessing children, we need to remember we are getting but a small glimpse of what any one child can do; growth is always further along than we can observe or measure externally.

The cognitive growth rate is most rapid between birth and about six years of age. Therefore, to get an accurate picture of where a child is in any one area at a specific point in time, we need to assess the child more frequently. This also makes assessment information less reliable in predicting a younger child's future performance than it is for older children.

Physiological maturation affects a child's learning and performance abilities. With young children, it is difficult, in many cases, to distinguish whether a slower rate of mastering skills is due to a slower rate of physiological maturation or due to some organic anomaly. This makes prediction of future performance based on current performance more difficult, if not impossible.

The external manifestations of learning and capacity to do things are directly related to the number and types of stimuli present in a young child's early environment. This can make it difficult to discern how much a child's performance in any one area has been affected by inadequate exposure versus a more organic delay in the child's development. Therefore, assessment conclusions for younger children, especially those of preschool age, should be viewed as more tentative in nature. The presence of educated and caring parents will often result in a child who is more precocious and better adjusted to his environment and to people in general. Others who appear to be slow starters may not have had the exposure to events or to people who could teach them and guide them in those early years. These children, given a similar school environment and a reasonable period of time, can often catch up to other students.

However, testing these children may erroneously classify and label the late starters. This is a situation we want to avoid at all costs as it will be at the expense of children who have not had access to a variety of early environmental experiences to the degree that many children do.

Purposes for Assessing Young Children

332. Working with children on a daily basis provides childcare workers and teachers with a wealth of information about a specific child. Documentation of what is known about a child by the adults working with him should take place prior to making an assessment of that child. This will help determine if and what additional information about the child is needed and what that information should be before an assessment process is initiated.

333. At times, a childcare provider or teacher may have questions as to the functional level of a child or the area in which a child needs extra instruction or accommodation. Assessing a child's performance in the area of question is appropriate for matching instruction, materials, and activities with the child's level of need, known as the zone of proximal development (see Chapter 1).

334. Some type of assessment is often needed to determine what progress children are making and at what rate they are making this progress. Assessment of the child's abilities from a documented starting point will provide an accurate accounting of the child's progress. Dates, how the skill or learning is assessed, and the materials that are used in making the assessments are important for an accurate measurement of a child's progress.

335. In cases where it is determined that a child is not making adequate progress, an assessment is warranted for the purpose of screening the child for developmental delays or possible disabilities that may require special attention.

336. Assessment for placement purposes (to see if a child meets special needs eligibility) is required when there is evidence obtained from screening assessments, documented lack of progress, and observations by the adults working with the child, and the child's parents that substantiates the need for this type of assessment. This would be considered to be a comprehensive assessment requiring the involvement and input of all adults working with the child, or child's parents, and professionals (such as special education teachers, psychologists, social workers, etc.).

337. Assessments are needed periodically to evaluate the effectiveness of the interventions for a specific child. These can be at the learning and/or behavioral level for children with or without special needs. Based on this assessment, a determination can be made as to whether or not a child's program needs to be modified.

Assessment Tools and Techniques

338. The selection of the procedures, materials, and criteria to be used in assessing young children must be done carefully and take into consideration the following factors:

- The area of development, skill, or behavior to be assessed
- The procedures and instruments that will provide the most relevant information with the least intrusion on the child
- The child's primary language
- The cultural background of the child
- The child's communication skills
- Conditions present that might have an impact on the child's performance (such as low vision or a physical disability)
- The person(s) doing the assessment
- The location where the assessment takes place

Observation

339. Observation of the child in his natural setting while engaging in routine daily activities should be a part of every child's assessment. This gives the best overall picture of the functional level of the child in many areas. This process consists of an adult watching the child, recording the actions of the child, and making intuitive assumptions regarding how the child feels about what he is doing. It is important to observe the quality of what the child does as well as his actions.

340. Observe children in a variety of situations. Some of these observations should be:

- Behaviors during routines (snack time, getting ready to go outside, cleaning up from an activity, etc.)
- How the child interacts with various materials
- How the child interacts with other children during play time and also doing more structured, hands-on activities
- How the child interacts with other adults

- The extent to which the child engages in solitary play and uses his options for independent activity
- How the child uses his solitary time
- Behavior of the child in a group setting when it is being teacher-directed
- General levels of performance in various areas of development, both in terms of what the child can do and in comparison to similarly aged peers

341. Write down the behaviors and the child's associated feelings as they occur by using charts and checklists designed for the appropriate age and developmental level of the child you are observing. It is best to try several methods for recording behaviors to see which one works best.

342. Observe children doing the same thing on a repeated basis to allow for the unpredictability of young children's behavior from day to day.

343. When you feel you have observed a child enough to be able to describe the behaviors and feelings the child demonstrates, analyze the data to determine the strengths, limitations, and functional levels of the child.

344. Look for patterns of behavior and feelings in the observational data you have collected about the child. Document these and use this information in determining goals for the child and how best to meet them.

Interviews

345. An interview consists of a series of questions or open-ended statements ("Tell me about Joe") that are used in accessing information about children from their parents and other adults who know and work with them. For the less skilled interviewer, it is advisable to use a more structured approach that consists of a series of specific questions created for the purpose of obtaining information about a child.

346. If you make up your own questions for the interview rather than using an appropriate commercial form, focus on using open-ended questions (requiring more than a "yes" or "no" answer) rather than closed questions (requiring only a "yes," "no," or single word answer). An example of an open-ended question is, "Tell me some of the things that Joey enjoys doing most when he is at home." An example of a closed question is, "Does Joey like to play alone?" Closed questions are appropriate for accessing some information such as, "How old was Joey when his sister was born?"

347. Summarize the information you receive from each of the adults you interview about the child. Look for commonalities and differences. Analyze the information from the interviews to determine if there are any consistent themes or patterns that have relevance to working with the child.

Standardized Tests

Standardized tests are created for the purpose of comparing a child's abilities or development in the areas of cognitive (thinking), emotional, social, physical, and adaptive behaviors to other children of similar age. These tests may be either *norm-referenced*, where the child's scores are compared to the norm or average behavior of similar age children (such as on intelligence and achievement tests), or *criterion-referenced*, which measure a child's skills relative to skills taught or skills needed to perform a specific task.

348. Standardized tests are most often required when screening young children for developmental delays or disabilities for diagnostic purposes, for placement purposes, and for measuring a child's progress relative to his peers. There are a number of these tests available. It is usually the person trained to give these types of tests that makes the decision as to which tests to use. If you have any questions regarding the options, consult the person who is coordinating the testing process or the person who will be administering the tests to the child.

349. Standardized tests consist of a series of items that require a specific response or follow a set of criteria that can be objectively scored. The norms for these tests are based on how sample populations of children of varying ages and grade levels have performed across the United States. Scores from standardized tests, such as the Kaufman Assessment Battery for Children, are most often reported as standard scores or percentile scores. Many of the developmental tests for young children also use age equivalency scores to report testing results.

350. When interpreting test scores, it is necessary to understand the meaning of the score used for reporting test results in order to draw accurate conclusions about the performance of a specific child. This makes your explanation to the parents more understandable and more accurate.

351. Standard scores are the most reliable test scores to use in interpreting the meaning of tests and communicating test results. Statistically, it is the most accurate representation of how a child performed relative to other children of similar age. Defined, a standard score is a score that has been normalized on a group of children across age groups.

A common number used to denote the midpoint of the average range is 100, give or take a few points for error in testing (the younger the child, the more error there is in testing). Any standard score that lies between 85 (+/-) error points and 115 (+/-) error points is considered to be within the average range. This includes 68% of the general population of children. Standard scores that are above 115 are considered to be above average and those below 85 are considered below average. Scores within these ranges can vary from somewhat above or below average to significantly above or below average.

352. For purposes of placement in special education programs, the quantitative standard score is most often used. For purposes of sharing information with parents, the terminology of above average, average, or below average is often used to convey how their child has performed relative to other children of the same age.

For every standard score, there is an equivalent percentile score ranging from approximately 1% to approximately 99%. These scores tell you the percentage of children who obtained higher scores and the percentage who obtained lower scores than the child tested. For example, if a specific child obtained a percentile score of 55 on a cognitive ability test, this means he did as well or better than 55% of the children used in the norm group. Furthermore, it means 45% of the children in the norm group did better than he did.

Given the fact that any percentile score between 25% and 75% is considered to be within the average range, this child scored at about the middle of the average range, demonstrating average cognitive abilities as measured by the test used. Percentile scores are easier to understand for adults who are not familiar with testing, but not as accurate statistically as standard scores.

Figure 5 below illustrates a comparison of standard and percentile scores as represented by a bell curve distribution.

A Typical Distribution of Standard and Percentile Scores

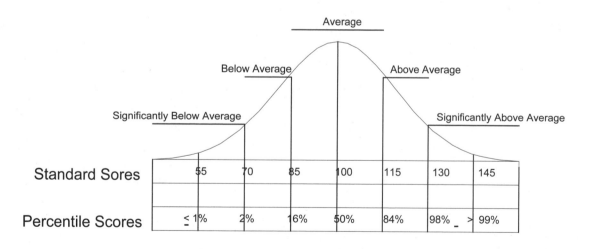

Figure 5

353. Age-equivalent scores are based on the performance of typical children at each age level. These scores are expressed as a numerical value by year and month of a child's age. Age-equivalent scores are easy to understand but are often

misunderstood. If you use these scores for explaining test results to parents, use them with caution. In most cases, it is better to use either terminology denoting above average, average, or below average, standard scores, or percentile scores.

354. Use standardized tests and test scores only in conjunction with the other information you have documented about a child from observation, interviews, etc. Remember, tests measure only a sample of behavior of a child for specific tasks in a given period of time. As such, it does not give the "whole picture" of a child. Information about how the child functions on a day-to-day basis at school and at home is necessary for getting an accurate picture of any child.

Other Assessment Procedures

355. A procedure referred to as Portfolio Assessment is gaining momentum in its use. With this approach, samples of a child's performance on a variety of tasks over a set period of time (such as a month) are collected and filed. At the end of the month (or other time period), these examples are shared and reviewed with the child's parents. This portfolio should contain samples of the child's best work. For children who need a great deal of assistance, you may want to label which examples were done independently and which were done with assistance.

356. Keep one sample of a child's work from each week of attendance. You may prefer to choose a sample of the child's art work, attempts at writing, or both. Be sure to date each sample, so that every few months you can look at these samples to evaluate the progress of the child in these areas. Include as many areas as you wish to track a child's progress. Sharing these with parents every three months is also an excellent way to keep them abreast of their child's performance and progress.

357. Creating simulated tasks that place children in a variety of situations can be beneficial in assessing children's functional abilities. This approach can be used whenever one is unable to observe and assess a child while he engages in these tasks in a natural setting or when a more detailed observation of the child is needed. For example, having a child sort objects and count them for you gives you an understanding of that child's knowledge about categorization and one-to-one correspondence.

Assessment of Children with Special Needs

358. Children with developmental delays and other disabilities need special consideration in determining what assessment procedures and tests should be used in order to get an accurate picture of their functional skills in specific areas. To determine the best assessment choices, consult with early childhood special educators and psychologists who are well versed in testing young children.

359. Testing of children with special needs requires a team approach where professionals can convene to decide on the information needed regarding a specific child, the assessment tools to be used, where the testing will be performed, and who will do the testing. Parents and childcare providers or teachers need to be members of this team.

360. Monitoring of a child with special needs (a form of assessment) should be an on-going part of the child's program. This should be in the context of the setting where the child engages in routine interactions and activities on a daily basis. Adjustments need to occur regularly as indicated by the results of monitoring the child's progress.

361. If significant changes are needed in a child's program for which there is an IEP (Individual Educational Plan), designated members of the child's team will need to convene. Parents and early childhood educators, childcare providers or teachers need to have input regarding the changes needed and to be clearly informed of what the changes will be.

362. There are many sensitive issues that challenge parents with children having special needs. Educators need to be alert to these and to be honest with parents about their concerns regarding the child. However, at the same time, it is important to be supportive of the needs of the parents and be aware of their level of sensitivity. Acknowledge and encourage the effort, love, patience, and care that the parents extend to their child.

363. When checking the progress of the children in your group, be aware of the limitations some children with special needs have regarding the demonstration of what they know through traditional assessment techniques. For these children, either use alternate assessment techniques or make the decision not to assess the child at this point. Discuss this with the child's parents and other members on the child's IEP team.

364. For children who have more severe disabilities, be especially selective in what assessment tools you use. For these children, the observations of parents and teachers along with informal measures of functional levels may be the most useful for programming purposes.

365. The National Association for the Education of Young Children (NAEYC) has published an excellent position paper regarding the assessment of children with special needs. This paper can be found in the book *Including Children with Special Needs in Early Childhood Programs*. This book is a must for your library if you are working with children with special needs.

Summary

Assessment is an ongoing process when working with young children. Being informed about the latest and best assessment practices is the responsibility of all adults who work with children in all school settings. This will ensure that assessments are always done with the best interests of the child in mind.

Children with developmental delays and disabilities will need to be assessed far more frequently and more critically than children without special needs. Adults who are sensitive to the needs of children, are knowledgeable about child development, and understand and love children for who they are can make these assessments a positive experience for children and their parents.

[Please refer to Form 16, 17, and 18 in Appendix A for supplemental information.]

Chapter Ten

The Future of Learning

Acknowledging the need for change in current educational practices is the first step in bringing about improvement. Embracing change is a challenge calling forth our creativity. What surfaces from this willingness to change will be the determining factor in the future of learning for children of all ages.

Curricula, materials, techniques, and beliefs that are no longer effective need to be discarded and replaced with more timely approaches. The new information that has emerged from brain/body/heart research can provide the means for accomplishing this challenging task.

Information is presently bombarding us from many different sources at an extreme rate of delivery. Our ability to function at this pace is no longer dependent upon how many facts we know, but rather on our ability to scan a broad array of information at any one time and choose which pieces fit into the "big picture." This requires problem-solving abilities that are based on a holistic processing approach as well as a linear approach.

Learners in preschool through high school will need to be given experiences and taught skills that will reflect this methodology. This requires a shift in our educational practices, which formerly emphasized a linear approach to learning and problem-solving, the memorization of facts rather than learning how to access information, and the reliance on external resources without an equal consideration given to one's inner resources.

These approaches may have served us well in the past, but they are decreasing in effectiveness to serve us now and will not be applicable for meeting the demands of our current information age. New data obtained from research on the human brain, new and more sophisticated technologies, and a better understanding of human interactions have opened up new options for educators to explore and integrate into the learning process.

Brain Research

The results of some of the new techniques used in brain research are providing more and more information about the organization and functioning of brain regions serving learning, language, social competence, and ability to pay attention. This is giving us new insights into the understanding of learning and attention problems resulting in new ways of addressing these challenges when working with children. However, the application of this knowledge is being extended to children on a limited basis at this point in time. More children will benefit in their learning environments once educators take it upon themselves to connect with this new knowledge, understand it, and apply it to the teaching process.

Knowledge about the brain/body/heart interdependence has expanded our options for working with children who have special needs. For example, medication and self-management techniques have been the primary treatments for children diagnosed with an ADHD or ADD disorder. Even though comparable success has been achieved through the use of neurofeedback, diet, movement, and auditory stimulation programs, these approaches have been used on a limited basis by parents and educators.

Evidence from brain science supports the need to pay more attention to the part that emotions play in the learning process. According to researchers such as Paul MacLean, Director of the Laboratory of Brain Evolution and Behavior at the National Institute of Mental Health in Bethesda, Maryland, and researchers at the Institute of HeartMath in Boulder Creek, California, emotions are vital to thinking processes.

Psychiatrist William Gray has proposed a model of the mind which says that "ideas are rooted in emotional codes" which he calls "feeling tones." These tones, according to his model, serve as vehicles through which rational ideas are remembered, associated, and reported. Does this mean that children may get more out of how something is being taught rather than from what is being taught (the content of the curriculum)? This whole area needs to be explored further relative to its implications for learning.

As Pat Wolf, an educator and presenter on brain research, has so aptly said, "emotions drive attention" which in turn "drives learning."

Nutrition and Learning

Recent articles appearing in the New York *Post*, ("Kids Ailing More and Learning Less") and in *USA Today* ("Kids Score C for Health") are but reminders of the increased concern about children's eating habits on a national level.

The scientific community has made us aware of the relationship between what we eat and the corresponding responses of our physical body. In educational circles, we have not paid enough attention to the effect of diet on mental clarity, memory functions, concentration, and behavior. The present concern regarding learning, attention, and behavior problems in our nation's preschool and school settings warrants a closer look at this issue. This needs to be done from two perspectives: the accessing of knowledge about the relationship between diet and the brain, and a dialogue about this knowledge can be applied by educators and parents to assist with the learning process and with the behavior of children.

Since preschool settings provide the foundation for children's future learning, it is critical for young children and for all children who are biochemically more vulnerable (who respond more negatively to inadequate nutrition) than other children to receive the most nutritious foods available.

Recent studies regarding the relationship between nutrition and learning suggest that many children who have difficulty learning and/or attention difficulties often have specific nutritional deficits. Correcting these deficits in some children has resulted in increased learning performance and concentration, which, in turn, concurrently impact the behavior of children. In some cases, the identified problem no longer exists.

It is important that all children get adequate amounts of protein, complex carbohydrates, essential fatty acids, vitamins, and minerals in their daily diets. When one of more of these essential elements are lacking for a period of time, learning and behavior are compromised.

An often overlooked requirement of the body and brain is its need for a continuous supply of water. Children need to be given the opportunity to have water bottles in their environments or an available access to water at all times. Studies have shown that the learning and behavior of children benefit from well-hydrated bodies and brains.

Other Needs of the Brain and Body

Children need adequate amounts of rest and sleep for the mind/body/heart to grow and develop the structures necessary for learning. In our fast-paced society, this need is often not met. This can result in states of imbalance in children of all ages. Associated behaviors of this imbalance can be observed as irritability, lack of motivation and concentration, and memory difficulties. Sleep is needed not only for the body to rebuild itself but also for information learned to be transferred to long-term memory. Rest in the form of "down time" and relaxation is necessary to balance the high levels of activity children engage in.

Recent brain research is helping to explain how movement directly benefits the nervous system. It has been found that muscular activities, particularly coordinated movements, appear to stimulate the production of neurotrophins, natural substances, that stimulate the growth of nerve cells and increases the number of neural connections in the brain. The number of neural connections and subsequent networks directly impact learning by integrating and anchoring new information and experience into these neural networks. Movement helps to awaken and activate many of our mental capacities which in turn increase learning and creativity. In addition, movement can also help release tension which results in better stress management. Knowledge of this type needs to be shared with all adults who live or work with children so that physical exercise and all forms of movement are an integral part of each child's day.

Environmental Factors and Learning

Over the past several years there has been considerable research undertaken in the area of learning ecology. However, this research does not seem to be understood or accepted in most educational circles. Researchers have investigated such ecological factors as light, color, air quality, sound, and space. For children who are environmentally sensitive, these factors impact learning to a real degree and, in some cases, contribute to their learning, attention, and behavior difficulties.

For example, fluorescent lighting used in childcare centers and in schools has been found to contribute to the activity level of children labeled hyperactive or ADHD. Studies involving the use of full spectrum lighting in learning environments support the need to consider this alternative lighting in children's learning environments. The use of improperly chosen colors in learning spaces (especially the excessive use of reds and oranges), distracting environmental sounds, poor air quality or circulation, and lack of a variety of spaces for different functions have been shown to contribute to children's difficulties. Even with children who are not as environmentally sensitive, learning and concentration are significantly enhanced when these factors are addressed by adults when designing learning spaces.

Barbara Meister Vitale, a Florida educator, has found over the past several years that the use of carefully selected colors with children can help them improve their reading and behavior. The use of color to enhance learning and help children with learning and behavior problems needs to be explored further by all adults who work with children.

Expanded View of Intelligence

For many years, a child's intelligence was viewed to be the measurement of his capacity to problem-solve using verbal, quantitative, and visual/spatial symbols. Psychologist Howard Gardner has expanded our view of intelligence to include nine distinct forms of intelligence. His original work included seven forms, which implies that our concept of intelligence is evolving and expanding.

Daniel Goleman's recent book naming emotion as a form of intelligence has further contributed to this expansion. Indications from the research of heart-mind relationship suggest that the next type of intelligence to emerge will be that of heart intelligence.

Adults working with children need to be aware of the difference in meaning between the words intellect and intelligence. Intellect generally refers to the cognitive aspect of thinking. Intelligence involves the intellect but is viewed through all behaviors involved in learning, social contexts, and life situations. The application of knowledge is key to understanding and using the term intelligence.

The amount of activity in the work of discovering and defining talents relative to intelligence challenges all of us to keep abreast of and be open to the implications of this knowledge in our work with children. Given this expanding view of intelligence, we can no longer support or value only the more limited, traditional view of intelligence. All the talents of children need to be understood, recognized, and valued to the degree that they will be nurtured and supported by those who interact with them.

Responsibility

Young children learn through imitation. Translated to all learning environments for children, this means that adults who choose to work with young children are responsible for modeling the types of social interactions and enthusiasm for learning that we want young children to imitate.

In addition to this, we are also responsible for providing a foundation of learning that will serve them well throughout their school years and beyond. To do this is going to take some serious consideration on our part as to what type of models we need to create for children and how these can connect them with who they are within the context of society. To do this we need to give consideration to the following ideas.

When our emotional, social, intuitive, thinking and physical selves are in balance, we feel better and are more effective at what we do. Children tend to do this more than adults do, but they need adult models and support for doing so.

There are several child development theorists and spokes persons that are worthy of consideration in developing philosophies and best practices for working with young children. We need to look for concepts that are in the best interest of children and for those that operate from an integrated approach representing a compilation of thought. No one philosophy, belief system, or conceptual frame-work can serve all children equally well. Theorists such as Piaget, Vgotsky, Erikson, and Steiner (to name a few) have made major contributions to understanding and developing programs for young children.

The more we pay attention to our own evolution as adults, the more we can create programs that honor the evolutionary process for children. As a part of this process, we need to look at new ways of expanding and applying the concept of viewing the child as an interaction of mind, body, heart, and soul. As adults, we need to act from this position of "wholeness."

Curricula based on the routine life experiences of children, their interests, and their developmental readiness need to be evaluated relative to our current practices. We need to ask ourselves the question, "Does placing emphasis on the learning of letters, words, and numbers while ignoring children's natural interests and readiness deter their joy and enthusiasm for learning?" This is not an either/or issue, but one of balancing elements of both that are consistent with developmentally appropriate practices.

Legislation, research, experience, and court decisions support the rights of all children to have equal access to any program and setting. Equal access means that all childcare centers, preschool settings, and school settings accept children along a continuum of learning and behavior reflecting a variety of developmental patterns and abilities. Are we doing what we need to do in implementing this right for all children?

As we make the commitment to do this, we will meet challenges. In working these through, we need to ask ourselves the question, "Are our choices for curriculum, materials, and methodology inappropriate for the child?" rather than "What is wrong with the child?"

How do we model and teach toward a balance of what is in the best interest of the individual within the context of community? First we need to discover what this balance is in various circumstances. Then we need to model the behaviors that embrace a balance for both the individual and group so that children can imitate our behaviors and eventually take on this practice themselves.

We need to use our hearts to help guide us, putting a combination of feelings and thoughts into action as we work with each other and with children. The unconditional love we give to young children will mirror itself exponentially. Options for bringing positive energy and creativity into learning are clearly present if we work toward integrating the heart and the mind.

Young children are the products of the present and the harbingers of the future.

Can we afford not to extend these gifts to all children equally in ways that support them for who they are?

Appendix A

Forms and Activities

Form 1

Profile of Development

Name of Child:_____ Date: _____

		A	R	E	A	S
D E V E L O P M E N T A L A G E		Chronological Age	Language Development	Large Motor Development	Social Development	Cognitive Development
	6					
	5.5					
	5					
	4.5					
	4					
	3.5					
	3					
	2.5					
	2					
	1.5					
	1					

Key:

C.A.	=	*chronological age*
Lang.	=	*language*
Large	=	*large motor skills*
Small	=	*small motor skills*
Cog.	=	*cognitive development (mental age)*
Soc.	=	*social development (social age)*

Form 2

Cycles of Learning

Example: Preparatory Writing

Awareness Phase: Create a learning center or set aside a space in your room where you can display a variety of shapes, letters, and words in different color media. Provide writing tools, paper, sand trays, paint brushes, and watercolors for the children to experiment with in making shapes and letters.

Exploratory Phase: Assign small groups (no more than four at a time) to the designated area. Encourage them to become acquainted with the shapes and letters by tracing around them with their hands. Then have them experiment with making their own shapes and letters with the materials you have provided.

Inquiry Phase: Have children share their experiences with you. Ask the children questions about what they have learned. Supplement the children's information by sharing with them other information about letters.

Application: Discuss uses of the shapes from which letters are made. Show how you can make names, signs, etc., by combining certain letters. Provide the children with an experience through which they can make their names or signs to put up in their rooms at home. Children who cannot use writing tools can make their name (at least the first letter) from clay or play dough.

Form 2 (cont'd.)

Note: This same format can be used for introducing children to new experiences, concepts, skills, etc., in any area of interest. To facilitate this process, you may wish to have several blank forms available upon which to write plans. Make it useful for you. Below is an example of a format that can be used.

TOPIC:_____ DATE:_____

Purpose:

Materials needed:

Awareness Phase:

Exploration Phase:

Inquiry Phase:

Application Phase:

Comments regarding success of activity:

Changes I would make the next time I do this:

Form 3

Behavior as a Function of the Interaction of the Child in His Environment

Behavior is the result of an interactive process that takes place between a child and his environment. What the child brings to a situation, event, or relationship, and what happens as a result of the interaction influences future behavior. Portrayed visually, it appears as follows:

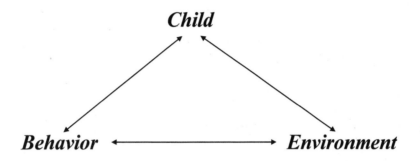

Example of Factors in Each Component

Child	*Environment*	*Behavior*
• Strengths	• Supporting, Caring, & Loving Adults	• Well - Adjusted
• Limitations	• Dysfunctional Adults	• Aggressive
• Temperament	• Transitions / Change	• Withdrawn
• Interests	• Trauma	• Fearful
• Vulnerabilities	• Experiences / Events	• Caring
• Personality	• Societal Expectations	• Affectionate
• Genetic	• Subculture Values	
predisposition	• Environmental Conditions	
	• Nutrition	

[Note: Words placed horizontally are not related across columns]

Form 4

General Strategies for Working with Young Children

Directions: Several strategies are listed below. Place two checks on the blank in front of the ones you are currently using. Place one check in the blank space for the ones you wish to try. After a period of two weeks, circle the numbers of the strategies that have been most effective for the child with whom you are working.

Child's Name:_____ Date:_____

_____1. Expectations for performance are consistent with the child's development and cognitive abilities.

_____2. Allow more time for the child to get ready and complete his activities.

_____3. Provide a quiet area where the child can go when needed.

_____4. Provide special seating when in a small or large group activity.

_____5. Filter out excessive noise or distracting sounds for the child when needed.

_____6. Adjust the kind and amount of lighting for the child.

_____7. Talk to the child's parents about the eating and sleeping patterns of the child.

_____8. Try the use of color for calming and concentration when needed.

_____9. Try adding music while the child is engaged in certain activities.

_____10. List additional strategies you wish to try.

Form 5

Categories of Modifications

Directions: Select one or more of the categories listed below that you wish to try for a specific child or small group of children. Under each category, list the interventions that you will implement. After the intervention has been used several times, mark the degree of effectiveness of the modification.

Child's Name:_____ Date:_____

Category 1: Adjust the demands of the activity. List the methods you will use to accomplish this.

_____
_____
_____
_____

Check the degree of effectiveness:

       Very   **Satisfactory**   **Not Effective**

   Continue the modification?   **With changes**
            Yes   **Yes/No**

Category 2: Pre-teach the skills needed for the activity. List the skills needed for the activity.

_____
_____
_____
_____

Circle the degree of effectiveness:

       Very   **Satisfactory**   **Not Effective**

   Continue the modification?   **With changes**
            Yes   **Yes/No**

Form 5 (cont'd.)

Category 3: Modify the expected outcome of the activity for the child. List the modified outcome(s) for this child.

_____

_____

_____

_____

Circle the degree of effectiveness:

       Very   **Satisfactory**   **Not Effective**

      Continue the modification?   **With changes**
                  Yes   **Yes/No**

Category 4: Provide an adult or peer (circle one) who will assist the child while doing the activity. List the assistance that will be given to the child:

_____

_____

_____

_____

Circle the degree of effectiveness:

       Very   **Satisfactory**   **Not Effective**

      Continue the modification?   **With changes**
                  Yes   **Yes/No**

Category 5: Plan a parallel activity for the child to do while the other children are engaged in the assigned activity. Make the parallel activity as similar as possible. Describe the parallel activity you will use.

_____

_____

_____

_____

Circle the degree of effectiveness:

       Very   **Satisfactory**   **Not Effective**

      Continue the modification?   **With changes**
                  Yes   **Yes/No**

Form 5 (cont'd.)

Note: **You may wish to combine modifications such as adjusting the activity and providing assistance. Keep these sheets as documentation of the modifications you have made for a specific child. After you have done this process with several children, make a compiled list of all the tested modifications for future use with other children who need modifications.**

Form 6

Creating a Personal Dictionary of Familiar Objects

Steps in creating a personal dictionary.

1. Provide the child with several pages of blank paper bound with a plastic spiral or some other form of binding.

2. Have the child choose the color of the paper he wants in his dictionary.

3. Have the child personalize the dictionary by having him decorate the outside cover.

4. Divide the pages of the dictionary into several sections. Start by having one page for each entry.

5. Start with the categories of common objects at school, favorite toys, favorite animals, and favorite objects at home. Add to these categories as the child is ready.

6. Present each object in the following sequence:

- *Give the child the object to look at, feel, and hold.*

- *For favorite animals, use stuffed toy animals.*

- *Have the child tell you as much as he can about the object. If he cannot tell you in words, have him demonstrate the use of the object with the object itself when possible, or have him show you by gestures or pantomime.*

- *Show the child a picture of the object while the child is holding the object. Use pictures that are cut and ready for pasting in the child's dictionary. Use words cut out of magazines that can be used as labels for the pictures in the dictionary, or write out the labels yourself.*

- *Tell the child the name of the object.*

- *Draw a rectangle on the piece of paper.*

- *Have the child paste the picture and name for each object into his dictionary.*

- *Present the child with a new object, picture and label each day, repeating the same sequence of steps.*

Form 6 (cont'd)

- *Each day when the child adds a new object to his dictionary, review the previous entries so that the child can build on his vocabulary, his recognition skills, and his understanding of common objects and their associated names in printed form.*

- *Tell the child the name of the object.*

- *Draw a rectangle on the piece of paper.*

- *Have the child paste the picture and name for each object in his dictionary.*

- *Present the child with a new object, picture, and label each day, repeating the same sequence of steps.*

- *Each day when the child adds a new object to his dictionary, review the previous entries so that the child can build on his vocabulary, his recognition skills, and his understanding of common objects and their associated names in printed form.*

[Note: There can be many variations on this process, such as using actions instead of objects, or varying the amount of work the child does independently or with assistance. This is an excellent project in which to involve parents or volunteers from the community.]

Form 7

Mazes

When working with young children, have them start out with very simple mazes before progressing to more difficult ones. When the children get familiar with how mazes work, have them create mazes for each other. Make a collection of these mazes so children can choose which ones they want to use. The child who created the maze will feel a sense of accomplishment and satisfaction through the recognition of having created something for others.

Hand-draw two horizontal parallel lines about 6 inches long (see below). Place the picture of two objects, animals, trees, or people at points A and B. Here is an example of this simple maze:

Encourage children to stay within the lines if possible.

Next, instead of two parallel straight lines, create your maze with wavy lines:

Next, combine parallel vertical lines with parallel horizontal lines to make the maze more complex:

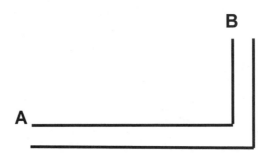

Form 7 (cont'd)

Keep adding lines and varying the shapes of the mazes as the children become proficient at the increasing complexity of the mazes. Here are some samples:

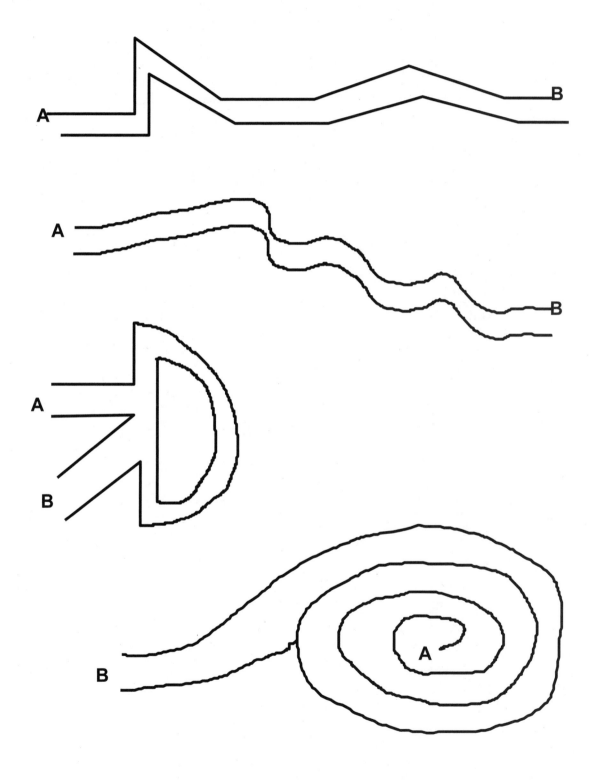

Form 8

Learning about Feelings through Working with Animals

Directions: Ask the children in your group to tell you what kind of pets they have at home. For children who do not have pets, ask them what their favorite animal is. Make a list of all the animals the children name. Lead the children in a discussion about how different animals show that they are happy, sad, excited, tired, mad, scared, and lovable. Compare the feelings animals show to the feelings children express by creating a chart with the expressions of the feelings of each type of animal. An example follows.

Expression of Feelings Chart

Feeling	*Child*	*Animal*
Happy	Smile	Dog - Wags tail Cat - Purrs Bird - Sings
Excited	Talks fast Gestures/body movements	Dog - Barks Cat - Tail moves back and forth Bird - Chatters
Tired	Yawns - Sleeps	Dog - Sleeps Cat - Sleeps Bird - Rests, Sleeps
Etc.	Etc.	Etc.

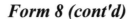

Form 8 (cont'd)

Continue this process until you have included all the animals named that can be fit into each of the feeling categories. Be sure each animal on the list fits into some feeling category. You can add to the feelings list as the children come up with new feeling words.

You can extend this exercise to talk about the qualities (other than feelings) of each animal. To make this more meaningful to the children, have them also think of the qualities they have, and which animals have similar qualities.

Depending on the age and abilities of the children you are working with, you can further extend this activity by having children draw their animal, write or dictate a few sentences about it, make up stories combining a number of animals, etc.

Form 9

Sharing and Talking about Feelings

Directions: Sitting on the floor in a circle formation is usually the best for this exercise. Introduce the idea of feelings children have by reading a story in which several feelings of the characters are shared through both pictures and words. List the feelings identified through the story. For each feeling listed, choose one child to draw a face expressing this feeling next to the feeling word. Then discuss with the children what it is like to feel this way, what makes them feel this way, and how they behave when this happens to them.

The second time you do this activity, introduce the idea of a talking stick. Explain to the children that only the one holding the talking stick can speak; everyone else must listen to that person without interrupting him. When the child is finished talking, he puts the stick into the middle of the circle, to be picked up by the next person to speak. The topic for this session should be a follow-up of the first session, by having children share times when they had one or more of the feelings from the original list. Then have children add any new feelings they have experienced, following the same format as in the first session. As children become more comfortable with this process, have the talking stick move around the circle to each child, allowing a child to "pass" if he does not wish to share anything.

This exercise should be used on a weekly basis at least. It will help children get in touch with their feelings, share them, and talk about ways to change uncomfortable feelings into more positive feelings.

New ideas about events, situations, and associated feelings should be introduced to children from time to time to continue expanding their understanding and expression of feelings. For example, a session could be created around the dreams children have and the associated feelings that they engender.

Bring color, music, and texture into sharing sessions as a way of helping children increase their awareness of how various stimuli in our environment affect their feelings. For example, with color, bring in several colors (paper, cloth, carpet pieces, etc.) and have the children look at and feel each color. Then have them share the feelings they had while looking and feeling each of the colors. Do the same with music by having them listen to different types of music to see which makes them feel calm, energetic, etc. For textures, bring in rough and smooth sand-paper, rough and smooth rocks, different pieces of cloth, plastic shipping bubbles, etc., and have them experience each through touch, describing the associated feeling.

Form 10

Learning about Feelings through Dramatic Play

Directions: Create a list of situations that parallel the experiences of the ages of the children with whom you work. Examples of these include:

- ✓ having fun with a friend
- ✓ playing with a pet
- ✓ falling down and hurting himself
- ✓ hugging a parent
- ✓ losing a game
- ✓ getting sent to his room
- ✓ going to the zoo
- ✓ getting into an argument
- ✓ getting pushed or hit by another child
- ✓ being called a name by another child
- ✓ having a birthday party
- ✓ someone accidentally breaking his toy
- ✓ a baby brother or sister being born
- ✓ losing a pet
- ✓ going on a trip

Start out by having children use puppets to role-play these situations. When doing this, it is a good practice to pair a situation with positive feelings and one with negative feelings so that children can experience the full range of feelings. When children are comfortable with using puppets for role-playing, have them volunteer play the roles themselves in each situation. Always allow enough time for children to process their feelings and think of new ways of expressing the various feelings that surface. Personalize the discussion as much as possible to fit the experiences of the children and their readiness to talk about them.

Use this activity periodically on an ongoing basis, encouraging children to add situations as they experience them in their lives, so they can continually expand upon their knowledge, their understanding of feelings, and their ability to express them.

Form 11

Learning about Empathy

Directions: It is often easier to help children experience what it is like to take the perspective of another child by first having them connect with the qualities and feelings of animals. The following exercise is one way to help children do this. Start out by choosing one animal and asking the question, "What would it feel like to be a_____?" Finish the question by filling in an animal's name and what the animal is doing.

For example,

What would it feel like to be a bird flying high up in the sky? on a calm day? on a windy day? when it is raining or snowing?

What would it feel like to be a fish swimming in the ocean? a goldfish swimming in a fishbowl?

What would it be feel like to be a deer walking in the woods? a mother deer walking with its fawn?

What would it be feel like to be a dog living with a happy family? a sad family?

What would it feel like to be a hamster living in a cage?

What would it feel like to be an elephant performing in a circus? walking down the street in a parade? walking in the jungle?

As children become familiar with this process, let them add animals and situations. Personalize this experience by having the children create situations involving other children and adults rather than animals. Use dramatic play to help children role-play a simulated experience. This brings feelings to the next level of understanding for children so that they can begin to feel empathy for other children and adults.

Form 12

Settling Conflicts Peacefully

Directions: Young children can learn to settle their conflicts when we give them a structure in which to do so. The use of a place designated as a "peace table" (or you could use a bean bag instead) is one way to provide a structure for children to settle their differences. This approach generally consists of two components.

Component One: A designated place that is kept specifically for children to use when they have a conflict with another child. Once the purpose of this place is explained to the children, have them help you name it. Make a special sign for this place.

Component Two: Guidelines for behaving at the designated peace place and steps to follow for resolving conflicts should be clearly posted. For young children who cannot read words, use pictures to convey this information.

An Example of Guidelines

✓ **Use quiet voices while in this area.**
✓ **Keep your hands and feet to yourself.**
✓ **Be as calm as you can when talking to the other child.**
✓ **Only one group of children can be in the area at a time and not be disturbed by other children.**
✓ **Let the children think up ideas to add.**

[Form 12 is continued on the next page.]

Form 12 (cont'd.)

An example of steps to use in settling conflicts peacefully:

1. **Use a spinner to determine which child will talk first (whichever child is closest to the direction where the spinner is pointing). The child who is not speaking needs to listen until the child speaking has finished what he needs to say. You may wish to use the "talking stick" idea for this process to help children remember that they can only speak when they are holding the stick.**

2. **Each child needs to take a turn in explaining what happened and how it made him feel.**

3. **Each child needs to respond to what the other child said.**

4. **Both children need to agree to end the disagreement or conflict between them.**

5. **Each child needs to offer one suggestion as to how they can avoid getting into a conflict if this happens again.**

The above components are offered as a way to begin this type of conflict resolution. It will need to be modified and adjusted, depending upon the age of the children and the types of conflicts they have. In any case, initiating such a structure will take several practice sessions with adult supervision for children to fully understand the process and what is expected of them for the process to be successful.

Form 13

Steps for Problem Solving

The following steps for problem solving may be used with a single child or with a group of children. Once this process has been taught and used, children will begin to use it independently or with only a slight reminder. Have the child:

1. **Tell what the problem is. If the child does not know how to describe the problem in words, have him find a picture that tells or suggests what the problem is, or have him draw one.**

2. **Tell how having the problem makes him feel. Again, if the words are not there, encourage the child to find a picture or refer to the feelings chart (which you should have in your room).**

3. **Tell you what he did about the problem. Brainstorm other ways of solving the problem. (You should add your ideas also.)**

4. **Choose one thing to do to solve the problem and tell you when he is going to try it. Encourage him to try it as soon as possible.**

5. **Tell you what the outcome of his actions from #4 were as soon as he completes the action. If the child is successful, celebrate. If not, go back to #3 and have the child choose a different action to take.**

Providing children the skills and practice to solve problems helps children become more independent and feel better about themselves. This helps children to lay the foundation for relying on their own resources rather than external ones.

Form 14

Steps in Changing Behavior

1. Identify the behavior you wish to change either to decrease a problem behavior or increase a positive behavior. Pinpoint the behavior by being as specific as possible, (i.e., hitting peers during play or at snack times).

2. Write down the goal you wish to achieve. For example, a short-term goal would be to decrease the number of hitting behaviors towards peers during play or snack time. A long-term goal would be to eliminate these behaviors.

3. List the steps you need to reach the goal (i.e., decreasing the hitting behaviors during snack times, decreasing the behaviors during play times, eliminating hitting behaviors during snack or play times.) Reaching a goal via several small steps is usually more successful than attempting to achieve a goal in a single step, especially for young children.

4. Establish a baseline (how often the behavior occurs now) by counting the frequency of the behavior during snack or play times for a period of three to four consecutive days. Record the frequency on a chart that is easily accessible. Golf counters work well for charting the frequency of behaviors.

5. Decide on the method and type of chart you will use for recording the behavior you are attempting to change. Determine the consequences (activity, social, or material reinforcer) that will help bring about the desired change.

6. Evaluate the effectiveness of your behavior management program by recording the child's frequency of targeted behavior over the set period of time. Then determine if there is a decrease in frequency compared to the frequency of these behaviors recorded on your original baseline. If the behavior is decreasing in frequency, your methods and consequences are appropriate. If not, you need to go back to Step 5 and make changes.

[For an example of a chart to use for recording the frequency of a child's behaviors, see Form 15.]

Form 15

Charting Frequency of Behaviors

Example 1: Record the frequency of behaviors for obtaining baseline data (the number of times a behavior occurs within a defined time period before an intervention is initiated) and the effectiveness of the interventions.

Behavior Frequency Chart

Child's Name: _____ Date: _____

Behavior:_____

Date	Activity	Time Interval	Number of Behaviors

Use one color for baseline data and a different color to record the frequency of behaviors once you have started the intervention. It is best to use one chart for each activity. However, if you wish to record more than one activity on a chart, use a different color for each activity.

Form 15 (cont'd.)

Example 2: Record the frequency of a child's behaviors to obtain base-line data and effectiveness of your interventions.

Behavior Frequency Chart

Child's Name: _____   Date: _____

Behavior:_____

	Baseline Frequency			Frequency of Behaviors with Intervention								
30X												
25X												
20X												
15X												
10X												
5X												
1	*2*	*3*	*4*	*1*	*2*	*3*	*4*	*5*	*6*	*7*	*8*	*9*

FREQUENCY

Day

Form 16

Child Observation Form

Directions: Record behaviors as they occur. To make this type of observation, use the following steps:

1. **Choose the activity that you wish to observe the child doing.**

2. **Place yourself in full sight of the child but not next to the child. If you are supervising the activity or leading the activity, carry a small note pad and pencil with you.**

3. **Write down what the child is doing when you start the observation, (i.e., participating with the others, off by himself, etc.)**

4. **Every time you observe behaviors that are specific to the child (where no other child is demonstrating this behavior), record the time and note what the child did.**

5. **Continue doing this until the activity is completed. When the activity is completed, record the time and the outcome of the activity for the child.**

6. **Analyze the data.**

[Form 16 is continued on the next page.]

Form 16 (cont'd.)

Form for Recording Behaviors as They Occur

Child's Name: _____ Date:_____

Observation Done by: _____ Position: _____

Activity Observed: _____

Time	Behavior
etc.	etc. - Add as many lines as needed

Analysis of Data:

- ✓ Number of minutes the activity lasted:
- ✓ Number of "different" behaviors observed:
- ✓ Number of times a "different" behavior occurred:
- ✓ The most frequently observed behavior was:
- ✓ List any patterns of behavior that emerged and label them positive or negative depending upon the effect on the child being observed or on the other children in the group.
- ✓ Make a note of other information you get from the data, such as the amount of time they spend on-task versus off-task.
- ✓ Conclusions drawn from this observation:

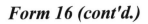

Form 16 (cont'd.)

Form for Recording Behaviors as They Occur:

Child's Name: _____ Date:_____

Observation Done by: _____ Position: _____

Activity Observed: _____

Time	Behavior

Form 17

Examples of Observation Forms

Example 1: Observing a child's degree of engagement in an activity.

Directions: After observing a child in an activity, use the following key to record the child's level of involvement in the activity.

1. **The child avoids the activity or makes no attempt to become involved when an opportunity to engage in the activity is given.**

2. **The child attempts the activity but seeks help or support in order to do so.**

3. **The child engages in the activity with satisfaction.**

4. **The child uses a variety of skills equally well when engaging in the activity.**

Child's Name: _____ Date: _____

Observed by: _____ Position: _____

Name/Type of Activity	*Rating (1-4)*

This is an excellent method to use in gaining information about the child's strengths, areas of interest, and areas in which he needs assistance and/or improvement.

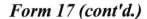

Form 17 (cont'd.)

Example 2: You may want to expand on this form by extending it and using it as a means of measuring a child's progress in time intervals. The appropriate time interval for young children can be either monthly or a minimum of four times a year. If used this way, the chart would appear as follows:

Name/Type of Activity	*Time Intervals*		
	Date/Rating	*Date/Rating*	*Date/Rating*

This method of observing and recording young children's behavior can be adapted to fit the purpose you wish it to serve and the information you need to access.

Example 3: There are some excellent commercial observation forms which can be purchased. The following Child Observation Record is an example of a comprehensive observation form for 2 1/2 to 6 year olds that can be purchased from:

High/Scope Educational Research Foundation,
600 North River Street, Ypsilanti, Michigan 48198.

Form 17 (cont'd.)

Child's Name: _____ Date: _____

Observed by:_____ Position: _____

Name/Type of Activity	Rating (1-4)

Form 17 (cont'd.)

Name/Type of Activity	Time Intervals		
	Date/Rating	Date/Rating	Date/Rating

Form 18

Interview about the Child

Child's Name: _____ Date:_____

Interview by: _____ Position:_____

How long have you known_____?

In what capacity?

Tell me about_____'s strengths.

Tell me about_____'s limitations.

What concerns do you have regarding_____'s learning? other areas of development?

Tell me about any health-related problems you have experienced in working with_____.

Is there anything else you wish to share about_____that would be helpful for the people working with him/her?

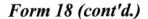

Form 18 (cont'd.)

Add any additional questions that you feel would be beneficial for obtaining additional information in working with the child. If you interview the child's parents, change the wording as needed. Also, add a question regarding the primary language spoken at home: does the child understand and converse in any additional languages? Ask if there have been any major changes, transitions, or trauma in the child's life that would be helpful for you to know about.

Appendix B

Bibliography

Baker, Bruce L. and Brightman, Alan J. *Steps to Independence: A Skills Training Guide for Parents and Teachers of Children with Special Needs, Second Edition. Baltimore, MD: Paul H. Brooks Publishing Company, 1989.*

Beaty, Janice J. *Observing Development of the Young Child. Third Edition. New York, NY: Macmillan, 1992.*

Berk, Laura E. and Winsler, Adam. *Scaffolding Children's Learning: Vygotsky and Early Childhood Education. Washington, D.C: National Association for the Education of Young Children, 1995.*

Bredekamp, Sue, Editor. *Developmentally Appropriate Practice in Early Childhood Programs Serving Children from Birth through Age 8. Washington, D.C: National Association for the Education of Young Children, 1987.*

Bredekamp, Sue and Rosegrant, Teresa, Editors. *Reaching Potentials: Appropriate Curriculum and Assessment for Young Children - Vol I. Washington, D.C: National Association for the Education of Young Children, 1992.*

Campbell, Don. *The Mozart Effect for Children: Awakening Your Child's Mind, Health, and Creativity with Music. New York, NY: Harper Collins Publishers, Inc., 2000.*

Chandler, Phyllis A. *A Place for Me: Including Children with Special Needs in Early Care and Education Settings. Washington, D.C: National Association for the Education of Young Children, 1994.*

Chenfeld, Mimi Brodsky. *Teaching in the Key of Life. Washington, DC: National Association for the Education of Young Children, 1993.*

Childre, Doc Lew. *Teaching Children to Love: 80 Games & Fun Activities for Raising Balanced Children in Unbalanced Times. Boulder Creek, CA: Planetary Publications, 1996.*

Cohen, Dorothy H. and Stern, Virginia. *Observing and Recording the Behavior of Young Children, Third Edition. New York, NY: Teachers College Press, 1983.*

Conners, C. Keith. *Feeding the Brain: How Foods Affect Children. New York, NY: Plenum, 1989.*

Cox, M.V. *The Child's Point of View: The Development of Cognition and Language, Second Edition. New York, NY: Guilford, 1991.*

DeGaetano, Gloria D., M.Ed. *Television and the Lives of Our Children: A Manual for Teachers and Parents. Available from Train of Thought Publishing, Box 311, Redmond, WA, 98073.*

Dennison, Paul E., Ph.D. and Dennison, Gail E. *Brain Gym. Ventura, CA: Edu-Kinesthetics, Inc., 1986.*

Elkind, David. *Images of the Young Child: Collected Essays on Development and Education. Washington, DC: National Association for the Education of Young Children, 1993.*

Forman, George E. and Kuschner, David S. *The Child's Construction of Knowledge: Piaget for Teaching Children. Washington, DC: National Association for the Education of Young Children, 1983.*

Gardner, Howard. *Frames of Mind: The Theory of Multiple Intelligences. New York, NY: Basic Books, Inc. 1985.*

Gardner, Howard. *Multiple Intelligences: The Theory in Practice. New York, NY: Basic Books, Inc., 1993.*

Gartell, D.J. *A Guidance Approach To Discipline. Albany, NY: Delmar, 1994.*

Getskow, Veronica and Konczal, Dee. *Kids with Special Needs: Information and Activities to Promote Awareness and Understanding. Santa Barbara, CA: The Learning Works, Inc. 1996.*

Goleman, Daniel. *Emotional Intelligence. New York, NY: Bantam, 1995.*

Hannaford, Carla, Ph.D. *Smart Moves: Why Learning is Not All in Your Head. Arlington, VA: Great Ocean Publishers, 1995.*

Hartley, Ruth E., Ph.D. and Goldenson, Robert M., Ph.D. *The Complete Book of Children's Play. New York, NY: Thomas Y. Crowell Company, 1963.*

Jensen, Eric. *Teaching with the Brain in Mind. Alexander, VA: Association for Supervision and Curriculum Development, 1998.*

Kagan, Jerome. *The Nature of the Child. New York, NY: Basic Books, 1995.*

Kline, Peter. *The Everyday Genius: Restoring Children's Natural Joy of Learning - And Yours, Too. Arlington, VA: Great Ocean Publishers, 1988.*

Konner, Melvin. *Childhood. Boston, MA: Little, Brown and Company, 1991.*

Koralek, Derry G., Colker, Laura J., and Dodge, Diane Trister. *The What, Why, and How of High-Quality Early Childhood Education: A Guide for On-Site Supervision. Washington, DC: National Association for the Education of Young Children, 1993.*

Kotulak, Ronald. *Inside the Brain: Revolutionary Discoveries of How the Mind Works. Kansas City, MO: Andrews and McMeel, 1996.*

Morris, Lisa Rappaport and Schultz, Linda. *Creative Play Activities for Children with Disabilities: A Resource Book for Teachers and Parents, Second Edition. Champaign, IL: Human Kinetics Publisher, 1989.*

Neugebauer, Bonnie, Editor. *Alike and Different: Exploring Our Humanity with Young Children. Washington, DC: National Association for the Education of Young Children, 1992.*

Ostrander, Sheila and Schroeder, Lynn, with Ostrander, Nancy. *Superlearning 2000. New York, NY: Delacorte Press, 1994.*

Ott, John N. *Light, Radiation, and You: How to Stay Healthy. Greenwich, CT: Devin-Adair, 1985.*

Parette, Howard P., Jr., Dunn, Nancy S., and Hoge, Debra Reichert. *Low-Cost Commuication Devices for Children with Disabilities and Their Family Members. "Young Children," September 1995.*

Pearce, Joseph Chilton. *Evolution's End: Claiming the Potential of Our intelligence. San Francisco, CA:1992.*

Rapp, Doris J., M.D. *Is This Your Child's World? - How You Can Fix the Schools and Homes That Are Making Your Children Sick. New York, NY: Bantam Books, 1996.*

Ratey, John J., M.D. *A User's Guide to the Brain: Perception, Attention, and the Four Theaters of the Brain. New York, NY: Panethon Books, 2001.*

Rich, Dorothy. *In School and in Life - The Best Gift You Can Give Your Child: Mega Skills. Revised Edition. Boston, MA: Houghton Mifflin Company, 1992.*

Samples, Bob. *Open Mind, Whole Mind: Parenting and Teaching Tomorrow's Children Today. Rollings Hills Estates, CA: Jalmar Press, 1987.*

Schlosser, Eric. *Fast Food Nation: The Dark Side of the All-American Meal. New York, NY: HarperCollins Publishers, Inc. 2002.*

Schwartz, Sue, Ph.D. and Miller, Joan E. Heller, Ed.M. *The New Language of Toys: Teaching Skills to Children with Special Needs - A Guide for Parents and Teachers. Woodbine House, 1996.*

Sobert, Mary A. and Bogen, Bonnie Neuman. *Complete Early Childhood Curriculum Resource. West Nyack, NY: The Center for Applied Research in Education, 1991.*

Stordy, B. Jacqueline, Ph.D. and Nicholl, Malcolm J. *The LCP Solution: the Remarkable Nutritional Treatment for ADHD, Dyslexia & Dyspraxia. New York, NY: The Ballantine Publishing Group, 2000.*

Vitale, Barbara Meister. *Unicorns Are Real: A Right-Brained Approach to Learning. Rolling Hills Estates, CA: Jalmar Press, 1982.*

Wolery, Mark and Wilbers, Jan S., Editors. *Including Children with Special Needs in Early Childhood Programs. Washington, DC: National Association for the Education of Young Children, 1994.*

Appendix C

Resources

National Organizations:

American Speech-Language-Hearing Association
10801 Rockville Peak
Rockville, MD 20852
800-638-8255   www.asha.org

Autism Society of America
7910 Woodmount Avenue, Suite 300
Bethesda, MD 20814
800-328-8476   www.autism-society.org

Brain Connection
888-358-0212   www.brainconnection.com

Children and Adults with ADD (CHADD)
499 NW 70th Avenue, Suite 101
Plantation, FL 33317
800-233-4050   www.chadd.org

Council for Exceptional Children (CEC)
1920 Association Drive
Reston, VA 22191
703-641-7824   www.cec.sped.org

Learning Disabilities Assoc. of America (LDA)
4156 Library Road
Pittsburgh, PA 15234
888-300-6710   www.ldanatl.org/

National Association on Mental Retardation
1010 Wayne Avenue Suite 650
Silver Spring, MD 20910
817-261-6003   www.thearc.org

National Association for the Visually Handicapped
22 West 21st Street
New York, NY 10010
212-889-3141

National Center for Learning Disabilities (NCLD)
381 Park Avenue South, Suite 1420
New York, NY 10016
888-575-7373   www.ncld.org

National Information Center for Children and Youth with Disabilities (NICHCY)
PO Box 1492
Washington, DC 20013
800-695-0285   www.nichcy.org

National Organization on Disability
910 - 16th St. NW, Suite 600
Washington, DC 20006
202-293-5960   www.nod.org

Schwab Foundation for Learning
1650 South Amphlett Blvd #300
San Mateo, CA 94402
800-230-0988   www.schwablearning.org

Contact these organizations for information on the state and local chapters.

Appendix D

Glossary

> *The words contained in this glossary are defined in the context in which they are found in this book.*
> *They are not meant to be complete definitions.*

achievement - *an accomplishment in learning or in the completion of a project.*

age-equivalent score - *a score based on the average performance of children at a particular age level; expressed as a numerical value, first by year and then by month of a child's age.*

assessment - *using informal techniques such as observation and formal techniques such as standardized tests to document what a child can do or what he knows.*

attending behaviors - *focusing and paying attention to a person, event, or task.*

behavior - *the visible expression and actions of a child.*

behavior management plan - *a plan of action prescribed for a specific child to decrease inappropriate behaviors and/or increase appropriate behaviors for a given situation.*

brain balancing - *using techniques or activities that engage the functions associated with both hemispheres of the brain simultaneously.*

children with special needs - *children with identified and documented disabilities or developmental delays.*

collaboration - *a team effort based on the idea of working together effectively and providing mutual emotional, mental, and physical support for one another.*

cognitive ability - *intelligence; one's proficiency in problem solving; one's capacity to think or to learn.*

cycles of learning – *a 4- phase reoccurring cycle that includes awareness, exploration, inquiry, and utilization which provides the foundation for the planning and implementation of learning experiences.*

developmentally appropriate practice *- educational practices that encompass both age appropriateness and individual appropriateness.*

disability *- impairment of normal functioning.*

distractibility/distraction *- the result of being easily influenced by external stimuli (such as visible objects, people, and sound) that take one's focus away from the task at hand.*

hyperactivity *- excessive activity in relation to others of the same age and in similar situations, often expressed as non-stop body movements or excessive verbalization.*

IEP *- see Individual Educational Plan.*

inclusion *- the practice of providing learning experiences for children with special needs in the same* <u>setting</u> *as children without special needs.*

individual educational plan (IEP) *- a written plan for the educational program of a child with special needs. This plan is developed by the local school in collaboration with preschool programs, early childhood programs, and K-12 school programs. Development and implementation of this plan must be in accordance with rules developed by the state the child resides in and federal guidelines. An IEP is written for a 12-month period and must be reviewed and revised annually.*

information processing *- the intake, mental manipulation, and output of words, symbols, and perceptions necessary to acquire new learning and to express or demonstrate this learning.*

learning *- any experience that results in a change of behavior.*

learning disability *- a condition in which a child is achieving and performing at a preparatory level or regular level in reading, math, and/or written language that is significantly below the expectation for his measured cognitive ability. This discrepancy must be due to difficulties in information processing rather than for environmental or other reasons.*

mistaken behavior *- behavior that a child engages in that is inappropriate for the situation.*

modifications *- adaptations made in the curriculum, activities, presentation method, or environment to provide support for the individual child to be successful.*

mental image *- the picture created in one's head to represent a word, symbol, or experience.*

motor development *- the growth of large and small muscles in the body needed to perform tasks involving movement of the various body parts, eye movements, and eye/hand coordination.*

percentile score *- a standardized score that tells how a child scored compared to other children. This score tells how many children (expressed as a percentile) scored above and below a particular child's score.*

psychological processes *- mental functions involved with taking in information, organizing it, transforming it, storing it, and using it.*

sequential processing *- taking in, organizing, and responding to information in a step-by-step, linear way where the order of the facts (information) is important in arriving at a solution.*

simultaneous (holistic) processing *- taking in, organizing, and responding to information all at once; seeing and relating to the "big picture" in which the information is randomly ordered.*

standard score - *a raw score (based on the number correct) that has been transformed to have a given mean (mid-point) and standard deviation from the mean. A common number used to denote the midpoint of the average range is 100 with a standard deviation of 15 points. Any test that has 100 as the mid-point and a standard deviation of 15 can be compared to one another.*

standardized scores - *raw scores that have been transformed to have a given mean and standard deviation based on a defined population used in the standardization sample.*

strategies - *techniques or tools to help one approach learning and problem solving in a systematic way.*

"time out" - *a technique used to redirect a child's behavior from inappropriate to appropriate.*

verbal abilities - *the understanding, manipulation, and expression of information and ideas in words.*

visual/spatial abilities - *the understanding and manipulation of material presented through the use of pictures, symbols, and models while also responding to their spatial placement.*

visual processing - *the understanding and use of information presented in pictures, symbols, or model forms.*

"whole child" perspective - *paying attention to and addressing the physical, emotional, social, and intuitive needs of the child in a balanced way.*

This space is for your notes

If you have questions or would like to request a catalog or place an order, please contact

Peytral Publications, Inc.

We will be happy to help you.

Peytral Publications, Inc.

PO Box 1162

Minnetonka, MN   55345

Toll-free orders: 1-877-PEYTRAL (877-739-8725)

Questions: 952- 949-8707

Fax: 952.906.9777

Or visit us online at:

www.peytral.com